SpringerBriefs in Finan

More information about this series at http://www.springer.com/series/10282

Erik Hofmann · Urs Magnus Strewe
Nicola Bosia

Supply Chain Finance and Blockchain Technology

The Case of Reverse Securitisation

 Springer

Erik Hofmann
University of St. Gallen
St. Gallen
Switzerland

Nicola Bosia
University of St. Gallen
St. Gallen
Switzerland

Urs Magnus Strewe
CRX Markets AG
Munich
Germany

ISSN 2193-1720   ISSN 2193-1739   (electronic)
SpringerBriefs in Finance
ISBN 978-3-319-62370-2   ISBN 978-3-319-62371-9   (eBook)
DOI 10.1007/978-3-319-62371-9

Library of Congress Control Number: 2017946024

This Springer imprint is published by Springer Nature
The registered company is Springer International Publishing AG
The registered company address is: Gewerbestrasse 11, 6330 Cham, Switzerland

Preface—Why This Book?

One of the most important factors of successful supply chain finance (SCF) programmes is the improvement of software and technology solutions that allow businesses to come together in partnership and speed up cash flows throughout the supply chain. Blockchain technology (BCT) promises to change the way individuals and corporations exchange value and information over the Internet, and it seems to thus be perfectly positioned to enable new levels of collaboration among supply chain actors. The first commercial application projects are already gaining traction, as technology giant IBM recently announced that it is teaming with one of the largest logistics service providers in the world—Maersk Line—to create a new solution to digitise the global, cross-border supply chain through BCT; China-based Dianrong and FnConn (a Foxconn subsidiary) have also announced the creation of a blockchain platform for SCF. These solutions aim to reduce complexity and make data sharing secure, accurate and efficient. Several start-ups are engaged in the area of blockchain-based letters of credit, bills of lading, factoring and reverse factoring to target the 'trillion-dollar' SCF market. Quite known are the start-ups Skuchain (https://www.skuchain.com/), Gatechain (http://gatechain.com/), Wave (http://wavebl.com/) and Hijro (https://hijro.com/). In the traditional letter of credit and factoring or reverse factoring, processing the compliance check is often still done manually by comparing the different paper-based trade finance documents, which causes cognitive exhaustion and high labour costs. Contrarily, string comparison in a digital document or cross-referencing entries (e.g. destination of the bill of lading is referenced in the letter of credit) based on smart contracts would reduce costs. This is where BCT comes into play.

This book aims to discover possible opportunities from the application of this fascinating new technology to SCF financing solutions, particularly in approved payables financing. In the first step, the principal barriers and pain points in delivering the financing solutions are identified. Then, a possible blockchain-driven supply chain model is defined. This framework will provide a basis for discussion on the relevant uses of the technology that could open up opportunities in the SCF space. The findings indicate that the blockchain and distributed ledgers technologies could deliver substantial benefits for all parties involved in an SCF transaction,

promising to expedite the processes and lower the overall costs of financing programmes. Furthermore, this book contributes suggestions for future research on the
topic of SCF and blockchain.

St. Gallen, Switzerland   Erik Hofmann
Munich, Germany   Urs Magnus Strewe
Origlio, Switzerland   Nicola Bosia
July 2017

Contents

Chapter 1
Introduction—Why to Pay Attention on Blockchain-Driven Supply Chain Finance?

> We should think about the blockchain as another class of thing like the internet—a comprehensive information technology with tiered technical levels and multiple classes of application for any form of registry, inventory, and exchange. M. Swan, author of Blockchain—Blueprint for a New Economy, 2015, preface

Bitcoin[1] introduced blockchain technology (BCT) as the first solution for transferring value and ownership of digital assets without the use of any trusted third party. In its simplest form, the blockchain is a shared database where all transactions of a given asset are registered in cryptographically chained blocks of data in order to become immutable. The system does not require any central authority or any single trusted third party in order to eliminate the related counterparty risk. Further improvements of this technology have allowed the running of small programmes (i.e. smart contracts), which potentially enable trusted automation of contractual relations between trading parties. If the Internet permitted the exchange of information between peers, BCT has made it possible to exchange value. The consequences of this technical revolution are difficult to foresee and will probably generate great opportunities for all industries and human activities.

All the largest financial services firms, for example, are planning to use BCT as a record of ownership and transaction in order to avoid the time-consuming reconciliation of each internal ledger in order to create a faster and safer system. Analysis suggests that this new technology could reduce banks' infrastructure costs attributable to cross-border payments, securities trading and regulatory compliance by $15–20 billion per annum by 2022 (Santander InnoVenture 2015). Currently, the two most prominent companies in this sphere are R3 CEV (www.r3cev.com), a New York-based blockchain fin-tech that is already supported by more than 50 financial institutions, and Ripple Labs (https://ripple.com), which is looking to establish secure, instant and nearly free global financial transactions.

---

[1] The largest transaction processed by the network is 150 million US dollars (Antonopoulos 2014, p. 4). On December 14, 2015, coidesk.com registered a peak of 216'251 daily transactions (coindesk.com 2016).

© The Author(s) 2018
E. Hofmann et al., *Supply Chain Finance and Blockchain Technology*,
SpringerBriefs in Finance, DOI 10.1007/978-3-319-62371-9_1

In addition to the discussed uses in the financial space, the open and distributed nature of blockchain seems perfectly positioned to enable new levels of collaboration across supply chain actors and enhance the integration of products and money flows (Saigal 2016). Camerinelli (2016), for example, suggests that at least one-third of the most common supply chain processes could strongly benefit from the features offered by BCT. These great prospects are therefore the motivator for the exploration of this technology. Particularly, as being located at the intersection of logistics, supply chain management, collaboration and finance (Hofmann 2005), supply chain finance (SCF) solutions could particularly benefit from the possible blockchain use cases and applications.

1.1 Purpose

The main purpose of this book is to identify possible opportunities for specific SCF solutions—i.e. approved payables financing (or buyer-led) techniques—triggered by the use cases offered by BCT. To reach this goal, it is fundamental to first present and describe all the different SCF techniques and processes in order to identify the current barriers, bottlenecks and pain points. At that point, two questions are posed

1. How can the application of BCT help to overcome the barriers of SCF?
2. What are the opportunities offered by possible applications of BCT in SCF processes?

By answering these questions, this book aims to identify which blockchain applications ('use cases') could create opportunities for approved payables financing solutions. SCF providers, investors and corporations involved in such financing programmes could be better positioned to make strategic decisions related to the adoption of BCT or the integration of any valuable application.

1.2 Structure

After a brief introduction to describe the purpose and the objectives of this work, this chapter provides a short literature review on the topics of blockchain and distributed ledgers and approved payables financing. Given that the technology is still relatively young and has only become prominent in recent years, there are limited reliable research papers and literature sources to reference. The informational sources needed for research will also include an analysis of documents beyond academic publishing (i.e. 'grey' literature). The literature review intends to give an account of what has been published so far, as well as an overview of the current status of the research relevant to the book at hand.

Chapters 2 and 3 provide a theoretical background on SCF with a focus on the different approved payables financing solutions and models (e.g. dynamic discounting and reverse factoring). As it is not discussed in the literature, the reverse securitisation instrument is described separately. In these chapters, the important terms, structures and processes are explained in order to identify the principal barriers and pain points in delivering and setting up a financing programme.

Chapter 4 gives an overview of the technical aspects of blockchain and distributed ledgers technologies in order to discuss the relevant use cases.

After having developed a theoretical framework, Chap. 5 provides an analysis of the existing and potential uses of the technology for approved payables solutions and the ability to deal with the barriers and pain points underlined in previous chapters. There, we aim to analyse other possible opportunities for SCF providers related to the mainstream adoption of the technology in the capital markets and supply chain communities.

The discussion in Chap. 6 will deal with the practical implications of the findings and the limitations of the research, and it will suggest directions for future research.

The findings are then summarised together in Chap. 7, where a brief conclusion will complete this work.

Figure 1.1 offers a graphical representation of the structure of this book.

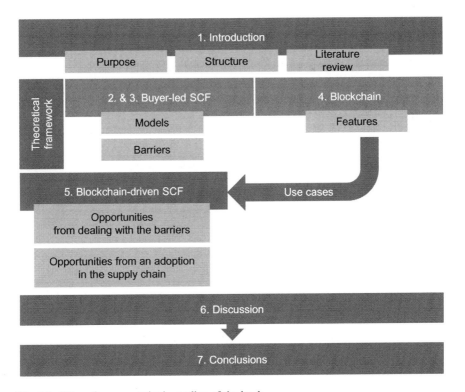

Fig. 1.1 'Line of argumentation'—outline of the book

1.3 Brief Look at the Literature

Because of the limited amount of available research that combines SCF and BCT, it was necessary to refer to the literature on the general topics of SCF, securitisation and BCT, which included industry related working papers, reports and online resources such as blogs and websites.

The seminal work that first presented the technical features of the technology is the white paper written under the alias of Nakamoto (2009). After Bitcoin gained popularity, research began to examine the discussions related to the technical features of this technology (Antonopoulos 2014) and its limitations (e.g. Dwyer and Malone 2014; Greenspan 2015; Sams 2015). Following the success of Bitcoin and the increased interest in this new technology, new solutions and blockchain 'designs' were presented in various technical papers that described the new features (e.g. Buterin 2013, 2015; Vasin n.a; Schwartzer et al. 2014). Later, the new Turing-complete blockchain feature fostered discussions on 'smart contracts', of which the principles were first described by Szabo (1994) and discussed in relation to blockchain solutions in research papers and blog articles (e.g. Flood and Goodenough 2015; Gendal 2015; Greenspan 2016). A broad understanding of the different blockchain designs, applications and use cases can be found in Swanson (2015). Once an overview of the technology's features and limitations was attained, a large group of research and working papers began to examine the different uses of this technology and its potential applications in a wide range of services and activities. Particularly relevant for our book are various working papers and industry reports that discuss the application of the technology in financial markets (e.g. ESMA 2016; Oliver Wyman and Euroclear 2016; Mainelli and Milne 2016; McKinsey & Co 2015; GBST 2016), for identity database management (e.g. Mainelli and Smith 2015; Biella and Zinetti 2016; Deloitte 2016) and for supply chain management (e.g. Bauerle 2016; Camerinelli 2016). Because of the pace with which developments around this topic occur and the topic's nature, the use of online resources such as websites (e.g. blockchain.info, bitcoin. it or coindesk.com) and blogs (e.g. 'gendal.me' or 'bits on blocks') were helpful in ascertaining awareness of the current status of this technology and obtaining some helpful thoughts and insights. Particularly challenging was the effort to not confuse the literature concerning Bitcoin with that examining the underlying technology (i.e. the blockchain).

Useful inputs for defining and describing approved payables financing (or buyer-centric) techniques were gathered from industry papers that describe the general SCF ecosystem and the key categories of SCF instruments (e.g. Aite Group 2014; GSCFF 2015; Templar et al. 2016) and from research analysing the SCF market and the financial drivers of companies engaged in such solutions (Hofmann and Belin 2011). Other contributions were made by Seifert and Seifert (2009), who underlined the principal differences between supplier- and buyer-centric reverse factoring models; contributions were also made by papers and articles that discussed the role of technology platforms as key enablers of such financing programmes (e.g. Leonard 2015; Zakai 2015). Key challenges for SCF are discussed in Camerinelli and Bryant (2014) and in an APEC working paper (2015), with the latter only specifically addressing regulatory issues.

Defining the reverse securitisation technique was particularly challenging because no literature was found for this specific SCF instrument. In order to define it, it was necessary to find support in research and papers that broadly cover the asset backed securities (ABS) instruments (e.g. Pfaue 2003; Fabozzi 2006) and, to further detail, the receivable securitisation technique (e.g. Mevissen 2005; Jobst 2008; Lussi 2009; Katz 2011).

References

Aite Group (2014) A study of the business case for supply chain finance. http://www.accaglobal. com/ab111

Antonopoulos MA (2014) Mastering Bitcoin—unlocking digital currencies. O'Reilly, Sebastopol

APEC (Asia-Pacific Economic Cooperation) (2015) Regulatory issues affecting trade and supply chain finance. http://mddb.apec.org/Documents/2015/SMEWG/SMEWG40/15_smewg40_007.pdf

Bauerle N (2016) Trade finance and supply chains. CoinDesk, New York

Biella M, Zinetti V (2016) Blockchain technology and applications from a financial perspective: unicredit technical report. https://www.weusecoins.com/assets/pdf/library/UNICREDIT%20-% 20Blockchain-Technology-and-Applications-from-a-Financial-Perspective.pdf

Buterin V (2013) A next generation smart contract and decentralized application platform. https:// ethereumbuilders.gitbooks.io/guide/content/en/whitepaper.html

Buterin V (2015) On private and public blockchain https://blog.ethereum.org/2015/08/07/on-public-and-private-Blockchains/

Camerinelli E, Bryant C (2014) Supply chain finance—EBA European market guide version 2.0. https://www.abe-eba.eu/downloads/knowledge-and-research/1406_EBA_Supply_Chain_Fina nce_European_Market_Guide_Second_edition.pdf

Camerinelli E (2016) Blockchain in the supply chain. Enrico Camerinelli

Deloitte (2016) Blockchain applications in banking. https://www2.deloitte.com/content/dam/ Deloitte/uk/Documents/Innovation/deloitte-uk-Blockchain-app-in-banking.pdf

ESMA (European Securities and Market Authority) (2016) The distributed ledger technology applied to Securities markets. http://www.the-Blockchain.com/docs/ESMA-DLT-Applied-to-European-Securities-Markets.pdf

Fabozzi F, Davis H, Choudry M (2006) Introduction to structured finance. Whiley, New Jersey

Flood N, Goodenough O (2015) Contracts as automaton: the computational representation of financial agreement. https://financialresearch.gov/working-papers/files/OFRwp-2015-04_ Contract-as-Automaton-The-Computational-Representation-of-Financial-Agreements.pdf

GBST (2016) Four scenarios for blockchain capital markets. http://www.gbst.com/insights/gbst-insights/four-scenarios-for-blockchain-in-capital-markets

Gendal R (2015) A simple model for smart contract. https://gendal.me/page/2/

GSCFF (Global SCF Forum) (2015) Standard definitions for techniques of supply chain finance. https://www.abe-eba.eu/Repository.aspx?ID=f7855005-f9b1-4b7e-bc4a-36ece3c9eb3b

Greenspan A (2016) Why many smart contract use cases are simply impossible. http://www. coindesk.com/three-smart-contract-misconceptions/

Greenspan G (2015) Ending the bitcoin versus Blockchain debate. http://www.multichain.com/ blog/2015/07/bitcoin-vs-Blockchain-debate/

Hofmann E, Belin O (2011) Supply chain finance solutions: relevance, propositions, market value. Springer, Berlin

Hofmann E (2005) Supply chain finance: some conceptual insights. In: Lasch R, Janker CG (2005) Logistik management—innovative Logistikkonzepte. Deutscher Universitätsverlag, Wiesbaden

Jobst A (2008) What is securitisation? Finance Dev 45(3)

Katz A (2011) Accounts receivables securitization. J Struct Finance 17(2):23–27

Leonard J (2015) Introduction to receivable securitization. The Secure Lender 2015(June):17–19

Lussi S (2009) Kapitalmarktbasierte innovative Finanzinstrumente für den Mittelstand—wie KMU dank dem Instrument der Verbriefung von den Vorzügen des Kapitalmarktes profitieren können. Verlag Dr.Müller, Saarbrücken

Mainelli M, Smith M (2015) Sharing ledgers for sharing economies: an exploration of mutual distributed ledgers (aka Blockchain technology). J Financial Perspect: Fintech 3(3):38–69

Mainelli M, Milner A (2016) SWIFT Working Paper: The impact and potential of Blockchain on the securities transaction lifecycle. http://www.zyen.com/Publications/The%20Impact%20and%20Potential%20of%20Blockchain%20on%20the%20Securities%20Transaction%20Lif.pdf

McKinsey & Co (2015) Supply chain finance—emergence of a new competitive landscape. http://www.mckinsey.com/industries/financial-services/our-insights/supply-chain-finance-the-emergence-of-a-new-competitive-landscape

Mevissen D (2005) Mittelstandsfinanzierung mit Factoring und Asset Backed Securities—Grundlagen Praxis Bewertung. Verlag Dr.Müller, Saarbrücken

Nakamoto S (2009) A peer-to-peer electronic cash system. https://bitcoin.org/bitcoin.pdf

O'Dwyer KJ, Malone D (2014) Bitcoin mining and its energy footprint. https://karlodwyer.github.io/publications/pdf/bitcoin_KJOD_2014.pdf

Pfaue M (2003) Strukturierte finanzierung—asset backed strukturen. Schäffer-Poeschel, Stuttgart

Schwartz D, Youngs N, Britto A (2014) The Ripple protocol consensus algorithm. https://ripple.com/files/ripple_consensus_whitepaper.pdf

Saigal S (2016) Supply chain finance and supply chain management will converge on the blockchain. http://www.tfreview.com/blog/supply-chain-finance-and-supply-chain-management-will-converge-Blockchain

Sams R (2015) Bitcoin blockchain for distributed clearing: a critical assessment. J Financial Transform 42:39–46

Santander InnoVenture (2015) Fintech 2.0 paper—rebooting the financial sector. http://santanderinnoventures.com/wp-content/uploads/2015/06/The-Fintech-2-0-Paper.pdf

Seifert R, Seifert D (2009) Supply chain finance—what's is worth? IMD Perspectives for Managers 178

Swanson T (2015) Consensus as a service: a brief report of permissioned, distributed ledger systems. http://www.ofnumbers.com/wp-content/uploads/2015/04/Permissioned-distributed-ledgers.pdf

Szabo N (1994) Smart contracts. http://szabo.best.vwh.net/smart.contracts.html

Templar S, Hofmann E, Findlay C (2016) Financing the end-to-end supply chain: a reference guide for supply chain finance. Kogan Page, London

Vasin P (no date) BlackCoin's proof-of-stake protocol. http://blackcoin.co/blackcoin-pos-protocol-v2-whitepaper.pdf

Wyman O, Euroclear (2016) Blockchain in capital markets—the prize and the journey. http://www.oliverwyman.com/content/dam/oliver-wyman/global/en/2016/feb/Blockchain-In-Capital-Markets.pdf

Zakai H (2015) Platform power: eeny, meeny, miny, moe—with which provider shall I go? http://www.txfnews.com/News/Article/5238/Platform-power-Eeny-meeny-miny-moe-with-which-provider-shall-I-go

Chapter 2
Background I—What Is Buyer-Led Supply Chain Finance?

2.1 Defining Buyer-Led Supply Chain Finance

SCF is at the evolutionary frontier of financial services that are closely related to the supply chain cycle (Templar et al. 2016). These services, mainly offered by financial institutions, leverage the use of documents, orders and contracts traded between companies, granting them to access to better payment terms and thus to a cheaper form of financing that generates liquidity and improves their working capital.[1] The Global Supply Chain Finance Forum proposes the following summarised definition of SCF

> SCF is the use of financing and risk mitigation practices and techniques to optimise the management of the working capital and liquidity invested in supply chain processes and transactions. SCF is typically applied to open account trade and is triggered by supply chain events. Visibility of underlying trade flows by the finance provider(s) is a necessary component of such financing arrangements usually enabled by a technology platform (GSCFF 2015, p. 11).

To better define SCF, we now discuss the three key elements of the definition: (a) working capital management; (b) open account (O/A) trade; (c) technology platforms.

Working capital management

In an increasingly competitive and globalised landscape, working capital control has become a key metric for chief executive officers focusing on profitable growth (Aite Group 2014, p. 6). Corporate clients can optimise working capital by

---

[1]Working capital (WC) represents the amount of day-by-day operating liquidity available to a business and is calculated as: $WC = (AR) + (Inv.) + (Cash) - (AP)$, where (AP) stands for accounts receivable, (Inv.) is the inventory value (raw material + Work in Progress (WIP) + finished goods), (AP) is accounts payables and (Cash) is self-explanatory.

© The Author(s) 2018
E. Hofmann et al., *Supply Chain Finance and Blockchain Technology*,
SpringerBriefs in Finance, DOI 10.1007/978-3-319-62371-9_2

managing to shorten its cash-to-cash (C2C) cycle, which allows companies to release originally locked up and idle capital to increase free cash flow (FCF), improve the internal funding ability and increase the enterprise value (Hofmann and Belin 2011, p. 7). The C2C cycle time is calculated as follows:

$$\text{C2C cycle} = \text{DSO period} + \text{DIH period} - \text{DPO period}.$$

The equation shows a clear conflicting situation between the trading parties: to shorten the C2C cycle, suppliers have to shorten their DSO (days sales outstanding) or DIH (days inventory held), while buyers have to lengthen their DPO (days payables outstanding). This means that by shortening the DSO or extending the DPO, the capital is tied for shorter periods, and additional liquidity is unlocked (Fig. 2.1). Due to the specular relationship that binds the trading parties, without the intervention of a third party, these two objectives are impossible to reach at the same time. SCF programmes release this tension, offering suppliers the possibility to be paid earlier by an external third party (e.g. banks or other investors), while the buyer has the possibility to pay at a later date. This approach allows both parties to improve the working capital and creates a win-win situation (Hofmann and Zumsteg 2016).

Open account (O/A) trade

Because of the intense competition for export markets, buyers often press exporters for open account (O/A) terms. For this reason, the world trade volumes have seen a dramatic increase in O/A transactions over recent years in front of traditional trade finance (Fig. 2.2). O/A transactions mean that the goods are shipped and delivered before payment is due (usually in 30–90 days). Open account trade entails lower fees and more flexibility than traditional forms of trade finance, such as letter of credit (L/C), bank payment obligation (BPO) or other bank intermediation products,

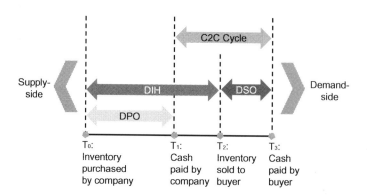

Fig. 2.1 The cash-to-cash cycle (Hofmann and Belin 2011, p. 7)

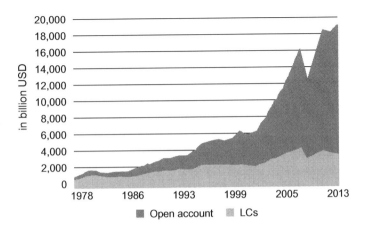

Fig. 2.2 Development of open account versus letter of credit volumes, from 1978 to 2013 (GSCFF 2015, p. 18)

but it leaves firms bearing more risk and a potentially greater need for working capital. SCF solutions are a direct response to this evolving situation (GSCFF 2015, p. 18), and such solutions offer the corporate clients involved in such trade flows an option for mitigating this problem.

Technology platforms

As underlined in its definition, SCF is usually enabled by technology platforms. One of the most important factors of successful SCF programmes is the improvement of software and technology solutions that allow businesses to come together in partnership and speed up cash flows throughout the supply chain as a result of the automation of processes (Camerinelli and Bryant 2014). While services have traditionally been provided by banks through their own channels and products, the market has been recently entered by fin-tech companies,[2] who are specialist financial technology firms that provide platforms and software-based services to support SCF operations (McKinsey & Co 2015, p. 1). These technology providers offer platforms that connect all parties together in order to facilitate the process of reconciliation, facilitate the exchange of purchase orders (POs), invoices, credit notes, payments and related information and facilitate the integration of this information between the different supply chain constituents (Hofmann and Belin 2011, p. 33). The importance of technology platforms was already emphasised in a study of Oliver Wyman (2008), which underlined that the typical client of a large SCF programme requires seamless integration in the client's enterprise resource planning system (ERP) and accounting package, while for middle market firms, the

---

[2]A McKinsey study (2015) estimated that 10–15% of the SCF market now involves fin-techs, and their growth is likely to accelerate.

bank's Internet-based trade platform is sufficient to successfully handle the financing programme (p. 19). The study also underlined that there are links between technology platform companies and banks in order to provide clients with the expected level of IT integration that they expect. Bank proprietary platforms that allow the information flow of the events that trigger the financing processes are often white label solutions of specialised SCF platform providers (p. 20). This is because many mid-sized and even some large banks have found it more efficient to collaborate with an experienced third-party technology platform provider than to try and develop an in-house solution (Leonard 2013, p. 63).

Table 2.1 gives an overview of common SCF platform providers (data: based on self-declaration).

SCF portfolio

All kind of documents, contracts and orders traded between members of a supply chain can be used to initiate a financing solution. Figure 2.3 illustrates the opportunities trigged by supply chain events starting from a good being warehoused and the respective issuance of a warehouse receipt until the invoice approval. The techniques can be classified as PO-based or invoice-based depending on the documents used as collateral.

In the case of inventory finance, the financing is usually confined to finished goods where a buyer has already been identified and for which a PO has already been issued. In this case, the financing party provides funds against the inventory (as collateral) or by way of a sale and repurchase agreement for the duration of the transaction. Similarly, with pre-shipment financing, the PO represents the evidence of repayment before production or shipping for the financing provider. The funds usually cover the working capital needed for the order's execution, such as raw materials, wages or packaging costs. Similarly, for these financing instruments, the intrinsic risk is higher than for invoice-based financing techniques due to the financing party being engaged in the very early stages of the transaction.

To date, invoice-based financing techniques represent the largest share, with an estimated 80–90% market share, whereas the remaining market share is held by inventory and pre-shipment finance instruments that are more specialised and not as widely practiced outside of certain industries. Depending on whether the programme is initiated by the buyer or the supplier, with invoice-based finance techniques, it is possible to distinguish between supplier-led and buyer-led financing instruments.

In a supplier-led architecture, the financing programme is initiated by the supplier and is set up to finance the receivables of the (any) vendor company. For invoice discounting instruments, the collection of the receivables remains under the control of the supplier, and the counterparty (i.e. the buyer) is usually not informed of the sale of the invoice (i.e. undisclosed assignment). The classical factoring or forfeiting instruments also fall under the supplier-led category, but the buyer is usually informed of the transfer of the title, and the collection is managed by the financing party (receivables purchase in Fig. 2.3).

In a buyer-led programme—approved payables financing—the liquidity is instead provided by the initiative of the buying party (i.e. 'reverse' factoring).

Table 2.1 Overview and characteristics of supply chain finance technology platforms (based on self-declaration)[a]. *Source* TXF Trade and Treasury, www.txfnews.com

Feature	CRX markets www.crxmarkets.com	Kyriba www.kyriba.com	Orbian www.orbian.com	Prime revenue www.primerevenue.com	Propell www.propell.co.za	Taulia www.taulia.com	Tower trade www.towertradegroup.com	Tungsten www.tungsten-network.com
Geographical scope	Worldwide	Worldwide	Worldwide	Worldwide	Multi-bank supply chain finance provider to buyers in Africa—and also service suppliers globally	Worldwide	Buyers based primarily in African sub-continent, Europe and North America. Suppliers are spread globally	47 compliant countries
Dynamic discounting	Yes—with discount fees determined either by the buyer or the supplier at a marginal financing cost	Yes—a flexible model responsive to the payment cycle of client	Yes—the supplier can elect to sell all approved receivables automatically or on a manual, ongoing basis	Yes—managed with minimal administration through the Sci Supplier platform	Yes—and suppliers can either elect to trade manually (full optionality) or on an autotraded basis	Yes—with suppliers either choosing manually from available payment dates or choosing to auto-accelerate all of their invoices	Not offered	Offer Tungsten Early Payment on an invoice-by-invoice basis, which allows suppliers to select which invoice they want paid and when. Platform allows users to visualise invoices and time them to match outgoing payments
Supplier onboarding	Onboarding is supported by electronic workflow on portal. Either CRX or the buyer liaises with the supplier	Provides the technology and send clients the user-guide. Buyer manages outreach to suppliers	Dedicated supplier onboarding team handles all aspects of supplier enrolment, including education and	Facilitated through Sci Enable platform, a link to which is sent by buyers to suppliers. Includes video tutorials,	Facilitated through an online, cloud-based solution	Varies depending on supplier sizes, from largest suppliers benefiting from face-to-face approach to automated email	This is carried out by the buyer's procurement team	Dedicated enrolment teams help buyer get suppliers on board and transacting

(continued)

Table 2.1 (continued)

Feature	CRX markets www.crxmarkets.com	Kyriba www.kyriba.com	Orbian www.orbian.com	Prime revenue www.primerevenue.com	Propell www.propell.co.za	Taulia www.taulia.com	Tower trade www.towertradegroup.com	Tungsten www.tungsten-network.com
			onboarding phase—working hand-in-hand with the buyer's team	messages from CFOs and interactive calculator		approach for smaller players		
Languages	English, German, French and Spanish primarily	11 languages, including English, Japanese and Mandarin	Most European languages, plus Mandarin, Cantonese, Japanese and Malay. Additional languages available on request	English, Italian, Spanish, French, Dutch, German and Chinese	English, French, Spanish, German and Dutch	All European languages and most widely used languages, including Chinese and Japanese	All European languages	English, Portuguese, Polish, German, French, Italian, Spanish and Bulgarian
Local currency financing	All currencies	Multi-currency	All tradeable currencies with observable Libor (or equivalent) interest rate curve	20, including GBP, USD, EUR and RMB	28, including USD, EUR, GBP, JPY, CHF, MXN and CNY	All currencies	USD, GBP, EUR, ZAR and CHF	All
Self-funding	Yes—either by early payment via Dynamic Discounting or by purchasing securitized notes	Yes—and often used by buyers in conjunction with Dynamic Discounting	Yes—through purchasing notes issued by Orbian after the purchase of the receivables	Yes—through a process in which the buyer is included as an investor	Yes	Yes—with a flexible model that allows them to self-fund when they have excess liquidity and allows the market to fund when they have alternative plans for that liquidity	Yes	Not currently available

(continued)

Table 2.1 (continued)

Feature	CRX markets www.crxmarkets.com	Kyriba www.kyriba.com	Orbian www.orbian.com	Prime revenue www.primerevenue.com	Propell www.propell.co.za	Taulia www.taulia.com	Tower trade www.towertradegroup.com	Tungsten www.tungsten-network.com
Funding sources	Yes. Dynamic Discounting, mult-bank and securitized notes. Funding can occur via a single source or multiple sources	A multi-bank platform, usually leveraging the corporate's relationship banks	All funding done via issuance of notes to bank and non-bank investors including buyer's own liquidity	52 funding sources, primarily major banks, but also capital markets investors and alternative financiers	Funding from multiple funders, local banks, trusts, capital markets and on-balance sheet funding from buyers	Partnered exclusively with Greensill Capital, which has an investment vehicle that allows multiple funding sources to invest in that vehicle—from buyer's house banks to hedge funds	Structured funds, retail and non-retail	Tungsten Bank, the invoice financing arm of Tungsten Corporation
Messaging	Messages are automatically broadcast to suppliers (e.g. rate changes) and to investors (e.g. auction announcements)	Not currently available	Automated messaging to buyers and supplier of all activity on account. Includes historic activity and alerts of pending activity	Directly facilitated on platform	Direct messaging in SciEnable, their supplier onboarding and messaging site	Integrated into the Taulia Supplier Portal. There are also message board for individual suppliers or globally	Yes, carried out through an internal electronic platform	Nor currently available
Financing rates	Two fee models: (a), fixed financing rates agreed either individually per	Use market rates drawn from multiple sources. Rates set either on individual	Set by agreement with buyer and supplier. They can be straightforwardly	Different financing rates by supplier, based on analysis of whole spend	Multiple pricing profiles can be setup for different buyers, supplier and currency	Set in conjunction with the buyer, using master-data to put suppliers in different interest	Charges levied vary dependent on the buyer	There is a one-off charge calculated according to the value of the invoice and the number of days until it is due

(continued)

Table 2.1 (continued)

Feature	CRX markets www.crxmarkets.com	Kyriba www.kyriba.com	Orbian www.orbian.com	Prime revenue www.primerevenue.com	Propell www.propell.co.za	Taulia www.taulia.com	Tower trade www.towertradegroup.com	Tungsten www.tungsten-network.com
	supplier or by supplier cluster; (b), based on an auction process	supplier level or for a group of suppliers (e.g., based on location or industry)	tiered for different suppliers		combinations. Financing rate for each pricing profile can either be Libor-linked (yield curve), linked to fixed reference rate or fixed (flat)	rates to each segment based on range of factors, including credit worthiness, ratings and own information we have about suppliers		(the charge decreases as you get closer to the due date)
Compliance checks	Yes. It provides a full-scale KYC support to purchasers where required	Carried out by banks	Yes—all compliance, regulatory and reporting requirements for each jurisdiction are fully supported and complied with	Collect and check information during registration—whole package for each supplier then given to the funder for own checking and approval	Yes. KYC, AML and regional compliance checks on behalf of all funders	Solution covers compliance required for the end-user	Carried out on buyers only. The checks on the suppliers are the duty of the buyer and/or the relationship bank	There is an internal KYC department that carries out stringent checks on all suppliers that are enrolled onto programmes
Analytics and reporting	Comprehensive reports are available either online on the portal and via xml or xls	Detailed reporting, tailored to buyer's requirements. Reports	Full suite of historic, and forward-looking tools for reporting and economic analysis	Issue reports that track and measure the success of a programme. Provide	In-depth spending analysis, term benchmarking, industry benchmarking	Taulia Analytics allows buyer to see suppliers who are on a programme, days they are	An analytics and reporting tool	Tungsten Analytics allows clients to access data and saving opportunities in real-time. Buyers

(continued)

Table 2.1 (continued)

Feature	CRX markets www. crxmarkets.com	Kyriba www.kyriba. com	Orbian www.orbian.com	Prime revenue www. primerevenue. com	Propell www.propell.co. za	Taulia www.taulia.com	Tower trade www. towertradegroup. com	Tungsten www.tungsten-network.com
		generated available online and for download		granular analysis	and supplier financial analysis	accelerating payments by, value of discounts they are achieving and so on		can quickly identify incidents of price variance for individual products and services across procurement activities, improving organisation's performance

[a]The information about the SCF technology provider is based on a questionnaire that was sent and filled out

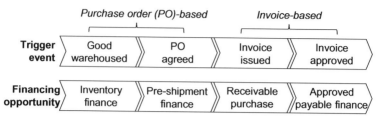

Fig. 2.3 Supply chain financing opportunities (adapted from Camerinelli and Bryant 2014, p. 136)

Although in both cases, the financial intermediary provides the funds by purchasing the receivables (i.e. the invoice with the embedded rights). Seifert and Seifert (2009) identified three important differences between these two categories: (a) Due to risk and volume issues, the focal company in a buyer-centric programme is normally a strong buyer. Thus, factors carry less risk and they can charge lower fees; (b) The bank has to evaluate only the buyer and finances the receivables of any supplier that the buyer cooperates with without worrying how creditworthy they are; (c) As the buyer participates actively, the banks obtain better information and can release funds earlier.

According to Camerinelli and Bryant (2014), payables financing instruments only account for approximately 20% of the SCF invoice-based market but have strong growth potential (p. 30). Figure 2.4 illustrates the SCF instruments portfolio.

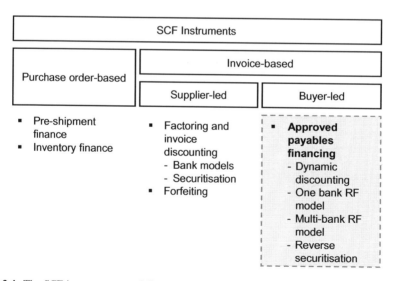

Fig. 2.4 The SCF instruments portfolio

2.2 Overview of Approved Payables Financing Instruments

As illustrated, buyers have the option to choose between different solutions to finance their supply chain and thereby their suppliers. In order to discuss possible blockchain applications, it is important to first understand which parties are involved and which role they play. This subsection describes the different approved payables financing instruments derived, as well as fundamental key drivers.

2.2.1 Dynamic Discounting

Dynamic discounting is a short-term financing instrument initiated by the buyer, and it offers to the buyer the opportunity to invest directly in its own suppliers, while suppliers have the possibility to benefit from an early payment of their accounts receivables (A/R) at a variable discount rate. Funds are typically provided directly by the buyer from its own liquidity resources. Dynamic discounting abolishes the formerly rigid interest calculations of an early payment (e.g. 2/10, net 30) and offers the possibility of a flexible discounting rate over the entire life cycle of the invoice. This solution enables suppliers to access cost-effective financing, which can be modified based on the current needs, while buyers can strengthen their supply chain and optimise their profits by collecting discount incomes, thus generating a win-win situation. Typically, dynamic discounting is most attractive for cash-rich buyers that do not have to focus on working capital as by paying the payables earlier to the suppliers the buyer's DPOs become reduced.

2.2.2 Reverse Factoring

Within a reverse factoring model, the approved payables can be bought on a platform by one or more banks (or legal entities that are permitted to purchase receivables), consequently offering a wider range of solutions to provide the early payment of the invoice. Corporate clients' reasons for choosing a multi-bank solution are to not be dependent on one single financial institution (Zakai 2015, p. 2) or to access to a broader range of financing opportunities that would be otherwise limited by the single bank commercial condition, geographical scope, product features or programme credit lines limit. A multi-bank programme permits the overhauling of the maximal programme limit of a single bank-driven SCF programme—corporate clients can then be served by another bank when the credit lines of an existing one have been exceeded, reaching a greater funding supply in a single programme.

Figure 2.5 illustrates a reverse factoring model with one or more banks acting as investors who finance the early payments. The starting point is the underlying

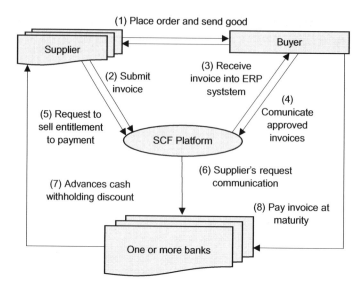

Fig. 2.5 Successive actions in a reverse factoring financing bank model

transaction between the buyer and the supplier (1). The invoice for the transaction is therefore submitted from the supplier to the buyer via the platform or any other form accepted by the buyer (2), enabling the buyer to receive it into its ERP system (3). As soon as the buyer has approved the payable,[3] the approval is communicated via the SCF platform (of the bank or other service providers) (4), allowing the supplier to see it. The supplier can therefore either choose to wait until the payment term expires and the buyer pays the invoice or decide to request the early payment from the bank (5). If the supplier decides to request the financing, the bank accepts the early payment request via the platform (6) and pays the invoice, withholding the discount (7). At invoice maturity, the buyer makes the payment to the bank for invoices that have been financed (8).

To protect the global financial system from being used for illegal activities by money launderers, criminals or terrorists, banks have to perform 'know your customer' (KYC) policies for every new customer (i.e. the suppliers) in order to undertake financial business with them. Identifying the customers and collecting the relevant information is a time-consuming and costly task, particularly for multinational corporations' programmes that have suppliers from all over the world. Given that a single KYC costs for a bank somewhere between 500 and 2,000 Euros in a normal case, if a bank wants to take part in a programme with 50 to 100 suppliers, the costs could therefore represent an important barrier. A survey from McKinsey & Co (2015) showed how the key to a successful SCF relies on the ease

---

[3]It is important to note that only eligible payables can be financed, submitted to a series of decisional constraints. For example, payables must be free from any liens or security interests and not have been previously pledged or sold (Alite Group 2014, p. 10).

of onboarding suppliers (p. 13). Also, a survey from ICC Global Trade Finance (2014) also points out how the principal reason for rejecting trade financing proposals relies on the burden of KYC procedures, particularly when dealing with foreign suppliers (APEC 2015, p. 35). Compliance requirements could thus be identified as one of the principal barriers in delivering SCF.

Barrier # 1 KYC requirements

2.2.3 Reverse Securitisation

This SCF instrument uses a securitisation technique in order to provide funds for early invoice financing. According to Katz (2011), given that receivables are typically the largest single asset category on companies' balance sheets, they are a natural choice for monetization through securitisation processes (p. 26). The pricing, transparency and structuring discipline of the capital markets should result in the best possible funding option for companies. It is expected that securitising the obligations out to the capital markets reduces the capital exposure for the involved parties, lowers risks and creates more efficient prices with benefits for the entire trade community involved in the SCF programme (Miller 2007). This provides smaller and non-rated suppliers with increased positive financing arbitrage and allows them to win bigger suppliers that have low marginal finance costs (CRX 2015). Securitisation programmes can also be carried out under a buyer-led architecture, and they are discussed in detail in Chap. 3.

2.3 Key Drivers of Approved Payables Financing Instruments

Beside the optimization of working capital for buyers and suppliers and the global shift to O/A, the motivations for the supply chain community and banks to enter in an approved payables financing programme are shaped by certain contingency factors. We now aim to identify the most important ones.

For small and medium enterprise (SME) *suppliers* particularly, liquidity represents one of the most dominant objectives for financing needs (Lussi 2009, p. 22). As identified by Altman and Sabato (2007), liquidity is one of the key financial ratios for measuring the riskiness of SMEs (i.e. the probability of default) (p. 5). A recent analysis of these indicators shows that they are falling sharply since the last crisis years, and by consequence, the creditworthiness of SMEs has been negatively hit (EBA 2015, p. 25). Even profitable businesses can suffer from liquidity problems, making them unable to invest in growth and development. SCF solutions offer the possibility for suppliers to deal with this problem and leverage the higher credit rating of the buyer in order to obtain lower financing costs.

For *buyers*, the increased risk of supplier's default has pushed them to adopt solutions to preserve the health of their supply chain while at the same time maintaining pressure for economies and efficiencies (Kerle 2009). Another key advantage for the buyer is that normally trade payables are not treated as debt for balance sheet purposes, which could bring a lower rate of financing over time due to unchanged debt-ratios. As reverse factoring reduces costs across the supply chain, some of the resulting value is captured by the suppliers, some by the buyer and some by the financial intermediary and service providers (Aite Group 2014, p. 15). Accounting treatment could, however, become a particular issue if the buyer wants to capture some of this value by sharing returns with the financing bank, which is also one of the main drivers for large buyers to initiate a programme. This operation can result in the reclassification of trade payables to bank debt and impact buyer's loan covenants, their leverage and their access to additional credit (Gustin 2014). Thus, a barrier in providing SCF is represented by the accounting treatment issue, which will be discussed in relation to possible solutions offered by blockchain applications in Chap. 5.

> **Barrier # 2** Accounting treatments

For *banks*, SCF represents an opportunity to deal with Basel III regulatory framework. Initially seen as a threat for trade and SCF solutions (APEC 2015, p. 39), the low risk profile and the inherent liquidity of trade credit solutions has made them an attractive asset class for dealing with the restricted capital ratio calculation directives imposed by regulators (Camerinelli and Bryant 2014, p. 87). As underlined by Leventi-Perez (2014), buyer-led SCF solutions are even more attractive because as counterparty risk shifts from suppliers to larger buyers with a better risk profile, banks can increase profitability as a result of lower capital requirements compared to other trade finance solutions. Another important motivation for banks to enter in a SCF programme is the lead generation created once the supplier has been submitted to regulatory compliance. Banks, then, have the opportunity to deal with a potential new commercial customer for any other product or business relation.

As seen, the rigid structure of invoice discounting can be eliminated using technology platforms that provide flexible solutions for exploiting the entire life cycle of the invoice, such as dynamic discounting. Usually, this option is adopted by cash-rich companies that can finance the programme without involving third-party investors (PwC 2014).

In the classical SCF model (i.e. bank-models), the funding is provided by a financial institution—usually the buyer's commercial bank—which sets the programme and finances the early payments at the supplier's request. Bank-created network approaches are likely to grow and find themselves as a preferred model.

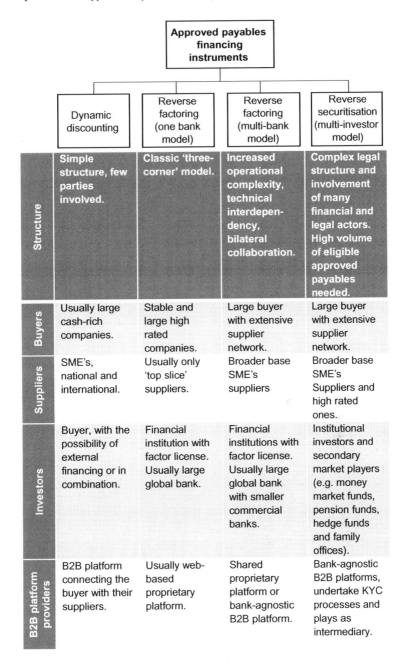

	Dynamic discounting	Reverse factoring (one bank model)	Reverse factoring (multi-bank model)	Reverse securitisation (multi-investor model)
Structure	Simple structure, few parties involved.	Classic 'three-corner' model.	Increased operational complexity, technical interdependency, bilateral collaboration.	Complex legal structure and involvement of many financial and legal actors. High volume of eligible approved payables needed.
Buyers	Usually large cash-rich companies.	Stable and large high rated companies.	Large buyer with extensive supplier network.	Large buyer with extensive supplier network.
Suppliers	SME's, national and international.	Usually only 'top slice' suppliers.	Broader base SME's suppliers	Broader base SME's Suppliers and high rated ones.
Investors	Buyer, with the possibility of external financing or in combination.	Financial institution with factor license. Usually large global bank.	Financial institutions with factor license. Usually large global bank with smaller commercial banks.	Institutional investors and secondary market players (e.g. money market funds, pension funds, hedge funds and family offices).
B2B platform providers	B2B platform connecting the buyer with their suppliers.	Usually web-based proprietary platform.	Shared proprietary platform or bank-agnostic B2B platform.	Bank-agnostic B2B platforms, undertake KYC processes and plays as intermediary.

Fig. 2.6 Spectrum of approved payables financing instruments

Two or more banks—or a pool of banks—allow greater flexibility and offer new possibilities for not only the trade community but also for the financial institutions. Banks can leverage potential for risk distribution with other financing partners or reach higher scalability by using specialised technology platforms. Clients and suppliers would then benefit from the price efficiency arising from the enhanced competition between market players.

Additionally, the payables securitisation technique allows the parties involved in a SCF programme to reach the higher degree of competitiveness, transparency and flexibility provided by the capital markets. The demand for lower capital cost is in fact seen as the most common characteristic of securitisation (Pfaue 2003, p. 169; Katz 2011; Leonard 2015). These premises create a spectrum of possibilities, which are illustrated in Fig. 2.6.

References

Altman E, Sabato G (2007) Modelling credit risk for SMEs: evidence from the US market. Abacus 43(3):332–357

Aite Group (2014) A study of the business case for supply chain finance. http://www.accaglobal. com/ab111

APEC (Asia-Pacific Economic Cooperation) (2015) Regulatory issues affecting trade and supply chain finance. http://mddb.apec.org/Documents/2015/SMEWG/SMEWG40/15_smewg40_007.pdf

Camerinelli E, Bryant C (2014) Supply chain finance—EBA European market guide version 2.0. https://www.abe-eba.eu/downloads/knowledge-and-research/1406_EBA_Supply_Chain_ Finance_European_Market_Guide_Second_edition.pdf

CRX Markets AG (2015) Case study—the power of securitisation

EBA (European Banking Authority) (2015) EBA Discussion paper and call for evidence on SMEs and the SME supporting factor. https://www.eba.europa.eu/documents/10180/1153414/EBA-DP-2015-02+Discussion+Paper+on+SME.pdf

GSCFF (Global SCF Forum) (2015) Standard definitions for techniques of supply chain finance. https://www.abe-eba.eu/Repository.aspx?ID=f7855005-f9b1-4b7e-bc4a-36ece3c9eb3b

Gustin D (2014) Supply chain finance payable reclassification issue—dead or alive? http:// spendmatters.com/tfmatters/supply-chain-finance-payable-reclassification-issue-dead-or-alive/

Hofmann E, Belin O (2011) Supply chain finance solutions: relevance, propositions, market value. Springer, Berlin

Hofmann E, Zumsteg S (2016) Win-win and no-win situations in supply chain finance: the case of accounts receivable programs. Supply Chain Forum: An Int J 16(3):30–50

ICC (International Chamber of Commerce) (2014) Global trade and finance survey: rethinking trade and finance. http://www.iccwbo.org/Advocacy-Codes-and-Rules/Document-centre/2014/ Global-Survey-2014-Rethinking-Trade-and-Finance/

Katz A (2011) Accounts receivables securitization. J Struct Finance 17(2):23–27

Kerle P (2009) The growing need for supply chain finance. https://www.gtnews.com/articles/the-growing-need-for-supply-chain-finance/

Leonard J (2013) Sharing the business. http://static1.squarespace.com/static/530ba8d7e4b0dd 985a47d576/t/531e0f96e4b0345bebdce093/1394478998171/Feb+2013+TFR+Article.pdf

Leonard J (2015) Introduction to receivable securitization. The Secure Lender 2015(June):17–19

Lussi S (2009) Kapitalmarktbasierte innovative Finanzinstrumente für den Mittelstand—wie KMU dank dem Instrument der Verbriefung von den Vorzügen des Kapitalmarktes profitieren können. Verlag Dr.Müller, Saarbrücken

Leventi-Perez O (2014) How Basel III regulations impact supply chain finance. http://primere venue.com/blog/basel-iii-regulations-impact-supply-chain-finance/

Miller A (2007) Trade services—pooled payables securitisation. http://www.gtreview.com/news/ global/trade-services-pooled-payables-securitisation/

McKinsey & Co (2015) Supply chain finance—emergence of a new competitive landscape. http:// www.mckinsey.com/industries/financial-services/our-insights/supply-chain-finance-the-emerg ence-of-a-new-competitive-landscape

Oliver Wyman (2008) The future of transaction banking volume 2. http://www.oliverwyman.com/ content/dam/oliver-wyman/global/en/files/archive/2008/Oliver_Wyman_Transaction_Banking_ Trade_Finance.pdf

Pfaue M (2003) Strukturierte finanzierung—asset backed strukturen. Schäffer-Poeschel, Stuttgart

PwC (2014) Managing risk: supply chain finance. http://www.pwc.com/us/en/risk-management/ assets/supply-chain-finance.pdf

Seifert R, Seifert D (2009) Supply chain finance—what's is worth? IMD Perspectives for Managers 178

Templar S, Hofmann E, Findlay C (2016) Financing the end-to-end supply chain: a reference guide for supply chain finance. Kogan Page, London

Zakai H (2015) Platform power: eeny, meeny, miny, moe—with which provider shall I go? http:// www.txfnews.com/News/Article/5238/Platform-power-Eeny-meeny-miny-moe-with-which-provider-shall-I-go

Chapter 3
Background II—What Is Reverse Securitisation?

3.1 Defining Securitisation in Supply Chain Finance

As illustrated, securitisation offers another option to finance obligations arising from trade relationships. This financing technique allows businesses to avoid the use of bank loans, capital increases or the direct issue of bonds and allows for credit to be provided directly by market processes (Jobst 2008). Although securitisation was initially used to finance simple self-liquidating assets such as mortgages, it rapidly became a common financing technique using all types of assets with stable cash flows, such as corporate and sovereign loans, consumer credit, project finance, trade receivables and individualised lending agreements, which fall under the name of asset-backed securities (ABS). An important difference from traditional supply chain finance (SCF) techniques is the way funds are raised: usually, funds are released by selling the income-producing assets (e.g. invoices) to a bank, whereas in an SCF securitisation programme, the respective pool of income-producing assets is sold at a discount to a special purpose vehicle company (SPV). The SPV then finances the acquisition by transforming the assets in ABSs and selling them in the capital market with its multiple private and institutional investors. Thus, securitisation approaches are also known as 'multi-investor models'.

We now consider the financing opportunities that arise from trigger events along a supply chain process, namely (unapproved) accounts receivables (A/R), buyer-approved receivables (commonly known as approved payables financing—APF) and inventory, which are working capital components (Fig. 3.1). No relevant literature was found to discuss the possibility of using purchase orders (POs) as collateral for securitisation purposes.

From a corporate point of view, in addition to offering an alternative funding source and all the benefits of a conventional reverse factoring programme, securitisation presents the following benefits:

© The Author(s) 2018
E. Hofmann et al., *Supply Chain Finance and Blockchain Technology*,
SpringerBriefs in Finance, DOI 10.1007/978-3-319-62371-9_3

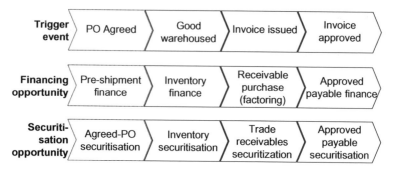

Fig. 3.1 Securitisation opportunities in supply chain finance as 'multi-investor models'

- As already underlined, the enhanced competition of the capital markets results in lower financing rates, particularly when the securities are offered in a book-building or auctioning process.
- Investors that are less regulated (non-banks) have no or fewer restrictions regarding capital backing and can therefore price more aggressively.
- The problem of maximal program limits of bank-driven SCF programs does not exist. Today, it is still expensive for corporate clients to add another single-bank programme when the credit lines of the existing one have been exceeded.
- Quicker supplier onboarding exists, as only SPV needs to perform KYC (in a multi-bank program, every bank needs to perform supplier's KYC). Moreover, the extent of the KYC requirements for Luxembourg originated SPVs, for example, is often far less extensive than for banks. This justifies the onboarding of smaller suppliers (activate the long tail of the supplier base) because of the reduced compliance costs.
- There are fewer transaction costs for investors, because instead of more complicated subrogation, only standard security settlements take place.

3.1.1 Supplier-Led Account Receivables Securitisation

In addition to conventional factoring techniques, accounts receivables have been financed through securitisation since the 1980s (Katz 2011, p. 23). Securitisation is an attractive funding source for suppliers because the key risk factor is the underlying portfolio rather than a company's balance sheet (Kerle and Gullifer 2013). Supplier-led securitisation risk is calculated based on the performance of the isolated pool of receivables. Therefore, the structure of invoice debtors plays a crucial role. Diversification is the key factor, since no ongoing credit assessment of the single obligor occurs; the receivables' risk, however, is calculated with

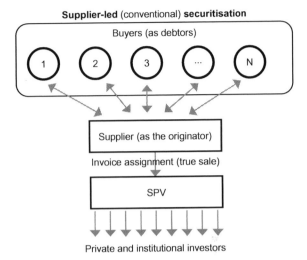

Fig. 3.2 Simplified originator–obligor–SPV relationships in a supplier-led securitisation transaction

aggregated past performances, and future cash flows are projected based on statistical servicing data (Mevissen 2005). From a theoretical perspective, issuers reduce the exposure to individual asset risk by holding a diversified portfolio through a spread originator's basis[1] (Figure 3.2). The underlying principle of asset securitisation is, in fact, that a large number of obligors in the collateral pool will reduce the credit risk via diversification (Fabozzi et al. 2006, p. 81). Furthermore, in conventional receivables securitisation, the counterparty—the buyer—is usually not notified of the sale of the invoice and is not part of the key players (GBRW 2004, p. 10).

Due to minimum size and maturity requirements, the acquisition of trade receivables is usually financed with the proceeds of short-term commercial notes placed in the capital market (Pfaue 2003, p. 169) known as asset-backed commercial paper (ABCP).[2] For this asset class, the transfer takes the form of a 'true sale' transaction, and invoices are normally sold without recourse (i.e. the originator —here the supplier—is released from further liability and does not respond with its assets in the event of a default of the transferred liabilities). In most cases, the collection service (servicing) is retained by the seller, because he knows his clients and the specific cases better (Katz 2011, p. 24). As noted in Fabozzi et al. (2006), servicing represents a critical role in securitisation transactions, and rating agencies and investors put particular emphasis on the ability of the servicer to perform the activities for which the servicer will be responsible for (p. 81).

---

[1]Mevissen (2005) considers that an optimal originator's pooled portfolio is composed by 200 to 300 obligors from different industries and geographical locations (p. 49).

[2]Usually from 30 to 90 days in maturity, rarely more than 270 (Fabozzi et al. 2006, p. 156).

In order to protect investors and obtain marketable high-quality notes, carrying out a securitisation programme can be expensive. The discount at which invoices are purchased must cover losses due to an obligor's default, servicing and program costs, and because trade receivables are non-interest bearing, it must also cover the interest on the ABCP notes (Rutan et al. 2003, p. 63). When structuring a securitisation programme, the objective is to offer the best possible quality of the notes issued in order to offer the cheapest financing opportunity (Mevissen 2005, p. 36).

3.1.2 Inventory Securitisation

A similar asset class emerged in the late 1990s in the form of inventory securitisation. Similar to other asset classes, this technique involves the sale of stock to an SPV and allows a supplier to raise securitisation financing when inventory is produced, rather than waiting until a sale to a trade customer (Moller 2000, p. 41). Similarly to trade receivables, inventory securitisations also tend to be completed through commercial paper conduits (p. 41) and under a 'true sale' structure (Gintz 2003, p. 264).

While inventory securitisation is usually focused on luxury goods (such as diamonds and champagne), other interesting candidates are assets in regulated and open markets, such as commodities. Still, according to Gintz (2003), the key factor is represented by high tradability and high durability (when possible with increasing value over time) of the inventory goods to be securitised (p. 265). Whether inventory securitisation techniques could be a viable instrument for financing supply chains is not discussed in the literature.

3.1.3 Buyer-Led-Approved Payables Securitisation

As anticipated, securitisation programmes can also be carried out under a buyer-led architecture, but it substantially differs from conventional supplier-led securitisation. Terms used to describe this approach are 'reverse securitisation' or 'approved payables securitisation'.

While in a supplier-led securitisation, the risk is calculated based on the performance of the isolated pool of receivables; in a buyer-led securitisation, the diversification effect is nullified, as all receivables have the same debtor—namely the buyer who gave the promise to pay. The credit risk is concentrated on one entity, which often is a large corporation for which the related risk can be clearly (and easily) identified and quantified (i.e. large buyers with investment grade rating). Figure 3.3 illustrates the simplified structure and relations in a buyer-led securitisation.

Fig. 3.3 Simplified originator–obligor–SPV relationships in a buyer-led securitisation transaction

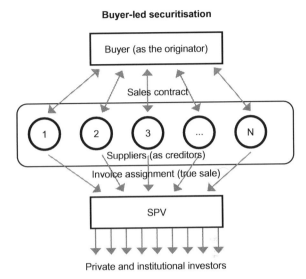

Buyer-led securitisation

Buyer (as the originator)

Sales contract

1 2 3 ... N

Suppliers (as creditors)

Invoice assignment (true sale)

SPV

Private and institutional investors

3.2   Key Characteristics of Reverse Securitisation

3.2.1   Structuring Options

In supplier-led securitisation, multi-seller conduits are common structures for conventional trade receivables securitisation (EBA 2015, p. 16) because they allow economies of scale to be reached and thus be a more accessible financing option for SMEs (Lussi 2009, p. 45). In a buyer-led programme, a multi-seller structure is given by its nature, and the single suppliers, as well as conventional reverse factoring techniques, can benefit from the strong credit rating of the buyer.

Multi-buyer structures (i.e. bundle invoice debt from a diverse set of buyers) exist for large bank-driven programmes (Miller 2007) but are more difficult to set up for fin-tech platforms. To reach an appropriate granularity in order to diversify risks, a minimum number of buyers (at least 20) should be required. The programme should then be able to finance every invoice requested by the seller; if not, suppliers would probably quit the programme.

Certain jurisdictions (e.g. Luxembourg) allow SPVs to be split into more compartments and thereby establish more than one securitisation structure within the same legal entity (PwC 2015, p. 12). Each compartment corresponds to the assets of a specific client (i.e. the buyer) financed by distinct securities and permits the isolation of them from the other receivables acquired by the SPV.

3.2.2 Credit Enhancement

In order to meet investors' risk profiles,[3] securitisation transactions usually use different credit enhancement instruments to increase the credit rating by trying to secure all the possible risks of an ABS transaction (Bär 2000, p. 194); this can be classified as external and internal credit enhancements (Fabozzi et al. 2006, p. 81). Internal credit enhancements are typically the subordination of notes in different risk tranches or overcollateralisation, while external credit enhancements are instead provided by external entities, such as guarantees from public support programmes, financial guarantee insurances or hedging instruments.

Public support programmes have been in place since the start of the millennium in order to stimulate SME securitisation. At the European level, the European Investment Fund (EIF), for example, is one of the leading providers of triple-A-rated credit enhancement in SME securitisations (Nassr and Wehninger 2015, p. 98), with a focus on the trade receivables asset class. It can provide various types of guarantees (such as wraps, bilateral guarantees, credit default swaps, etc.) on senior and/or junior tranches, typically with a minimum rating equivalent to BB/Ba2.

SCF programmes do not utilise tranches or external support. It is the aim of buyer-led securitisations to reflect the obligor's risk through the obligor's approval of the participating supplier invoices. This buyer approval is also called 'promise to pay'. It expresses that the buyer (the debtor) will pay the SPV (the new owner of the receivables) on first demand without recourse. Therefore, the supplier receives a credit enhancement in cases where the buyer's credit rating is better than the supplier's own.

3.2.3 Securities Issuance

As SPVs are able to issue an array of different debt instruments with precise risk and return characteristics, issuers have different options when issuing securities in order to finance the purchase of trade receivables. As mentioned, for the trade receivables asset class, the funding options are usually short-term securities—such as commercial papers (Pfaue 2003; Mevissen 2005)—as the matching of underlying assets and liability side (i.e. no maturity transformation) is seen as a contributing factor to qualitative securities programmes (EBA 2014, p. 47).

When it comes to accessing funding, it is possible to distinguish between private and public placements of the issued securities. Private placements address a limited

---

[3]As a general rule, only investment grade rated debt is purchased by the majority of funds, pension funds and retail investors (ERT 2014, p.42).

number of investors[4] and are submitted to less regulation and formal requirements, such as the publication of securities prospectus (Schlitt 2014, p. 66) or the formal credit rating required for publicly traded debt (Nassr and Wehninger 2015, p. 173).

Contrary to supplier-led securitisation, today, public placements for reverse securitisation do not exist for the following reasons:

- The buyer wants to have control over who can buy his notes and he is not interested in transparency (e.g. how investors do price the corporate risk).
- The volume of each transaction needs to be fairly high in order to compensate for transaction costs (e.g. a minimal investment amount of EUR 1 Mio. is required).
- A listing on a public stock exchange would be needed because a proprietary platform could not manage retail investors with the embedded regulatory requirements.
- A prospectus needs to be produced, which would result in high legal structuring costs.
- Having a heterogeneous pool of institutional investors (e.g. greater than 10) is sufficient to achieve aggressive competition.

3.2.4 Parties Involved

As mentioned, the advantage of reverse securitisations is that an external credit rating of the SCF securitization programme is not needed because there is no public issuance and the risk is easily identifiable (i.e. the buyer's credit risk). Despite avoiding the involvement of external rating agencies, the complex structure of a securitisation involves many other parties in addition to the parties directly involved in the SCF transactions (i.e. buyer, supplier and the investors).

With the rise of technology platforms, securitisation financing can in part overhaul a domain that has traditionally been ruled by specialised banks and offer a simpler and more flexible solution more suited to SMEs. Besides acting as the operator of the platform and ensuring that such proposed receivables comply with a list of eligibility criteria, such operating platforms, as Hatton (2015) points out, could also take all steps necessary to formalise any of the property of such receivables to the relevant investor, transfer the purchase price to the supplier and transfer the collections to such investors acting as *servicer*. Usually, this latter task is performed by the asset's originator, and it is usually compensated with fixed servicing fees. Another task performed by such fin-techs is the arrangement of the transaction structure and the invoice bundling for the note's origination (CRX

---

[4]Under German Law (WpPG), a placement is qualified as private if securities are offered only to institutional investors or to a maximum of 150 non-qualified investors (Schlitt 2014, p. 66).

Markets 2015). At this point, the securities' static data (i.e. an ISIN-Number) is distributed via an information service provider, and the note's terms and conditions are sent to a *central securities depository* (*CSD*) for the origination.

The securities post-trade process begins after the investor receives confirmation of an executed trade from the platform provider. Herein, a *custodian* bank settles the payments to the investors versus the issued securities, a process that needs the intervention of a CSD. Custodians are the banks responsible for safekeeping the securitisation vehicle's liquid assets and transferable securities, keeping the documentation that provides the existence of the securitised assets and ensuring that these are kept under the best conditions for the investors. There is a need for services from an information service provider (e.g. WM-Daten Services for providing ISINs for German issues), a CSD or clearinghouse (e.g. Clearstream Banking Frankfurt or Euroclear for European markets), or a custodian bank in order to manage the issuing and post-trade processes, and the actual settlement standards (T + 2 or T + 3) that tie up capital have a negative impact on the transaction costs. Because of the many parties involved in setting up the securitisation structure and the ongoing issuance of the securities, a high volume of eligible payments is required in order to benefit from the programme. The high transaction costs for establishing a securitisation structure and the entire post-trade process are seen as another barrier in delivering SCF, and this will be discussed in relation to BCT in Chap. 5.

> **Barrier # 3** High transaction costs

Finally, the *trustee* is the entity who is primarily concerned with preserving investor's rights (the responsibilities are described in a separate trust agreement). More generally, a trustee supervises the receipt and disbursement of cash flow and monitors the other parties under the agreement to ensure that they are compliant with appropriate covenants.

3.3 A Platform-Driven Reverse Securitisation Approach

Figure 3.4 illustrates a technology platform-driven buyer-led securitisation approach (from CRX Markets 2015). The starting point is the underlying trade between the buyer and the supplier. The invoice for the transaction is therefore submitted from the supplier to the buyer (1). As soon as the buyer has approved the payable[5] (2), the supplier can either choose to wait until the payment term expires

---

[5]It is important to note that only eligible payables can be financed, and they are submitted to a series of decision constraints. For example, payables must be free from any liens or security interests and must not have been previously pledged or sold (Alite Group 2014, p. 10).

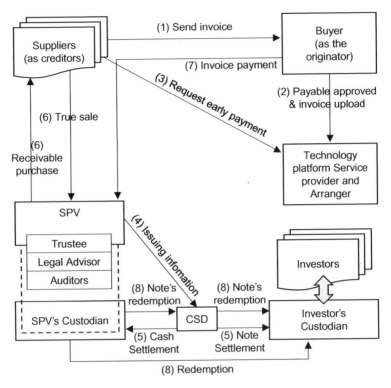

Fig. 3.4 Successive actions in a buyer-led securitisation transaction (adapted from CRX Markets 2015)

and the buyer pays the invoice, or decides to request the 'early payment' (i.e. finance via the SPV) (3). If the supplier decides to request the early payment, the issuing and paying agent receive the issuing information (registration criteria) from the service provider (which can be the arranger) (4) and issue a new commercial paper or note via a central securities depository (CSD) (5). If securities are successfully settled (which typically occurs in two or three business days after trade), payments to the supplier (originator) will be instructed by the SPV with the discounted invoice amount. The successful securities settlement is the condition precedent for the assignment of the receivable from the supplier to the SPV (6). When the agreed payment term between the supplier and the buyer expires, the buyer makes the payment to the owner of the invoice (i.e. SPV) (7). At the securities' maturity, the SPV redeems principal and interest on the issued securities (8).

References

Aite Group (2014) A study of the business case for supply chain finance. http://www.accaglobal. com/ab111

Bär HP (2000) Asset securitisation—Die Verbriefung von Finanzaktiven als innovative Finanzierungstechnik und neue Herausforderungen für Banken. In: Lussi S (2009) Kapitalmarktbasierte innovative Finanzinstrumente für den Mittelstand—wie KMU dank dem Instrument der Verbriefung von den Vorzügen des Kapitalmarktes profitieren können. Saarbrücken, Verlag Dr. Müller

CRX Markets AG (2015) Case study—the power of securitisation

ERT (European Round Table) (2014) Roundtable between bankers and SME's—SME securitisation. Final Report 204. http://ec.europa.eu/DocsRoom/documents/3345/attachments/1/translations/en/renditions/pdf

EBA (European Banking Authority) (2014) Report on qualifying securitisation—response to the commission's call for advice of January 2014 on long-term financing. https://www.eba.europa.eu/documents/10180/950548/EBA+report+on+qualifying+securitisation.pdf

EBA (European Banking Authority) (2015) EBA Discussion Paper and Call for Evidence on SMEs and the SME Supporting Factor. https://www.eba.europa.eu/documents/10180/1153414/EBA-DP-2015-02+Discussion+Paper+on+SME.pdf

Fabozzi F, Davis H, Choudry M (2006) Introduction to structured finance. Whiley, New Jersey

GBRW (2004) Study on asset based securities: impact and use of ABS on SME finance. http://ec.europa.eu/DocsRoom/documents/3342/attachments/1/translations/en/renditions/pdf

Gintz C (2003) In: Fabozzi FJ, Choudry M (eds) The handbook of European structured financial products. Wiley, New York, pp 263–270

Hatton V (2015) Securitisation and "Fintechs"—a material stake for future financings in France. http://www.lexology.com/library/detail.aspx?g=17691092-ba14-40d9-be57-b0823f296345

Jobst A (2008) What is securitisation? Finance Dev

Katz A (2011) Accounts receivables securitization. J Struct Finance 17(2):23–27

Kerle P, Gullifer L (2013) The future of trade receivables securitisation in Europe. J Struct Finance 19(1):71–76

Lussi S (2009) Kapitalmarktbasierte innovative Finanzinstrumente für den Mittelstand—wie KMU dank dem Instrument der Verbriefung von den Vorzügen des Kapitalmarktes profitieren können. Verlag Dr.Müller, Saarbrücken

Mevissen D (2005) Mittelstandsfinanzierung mit Factoring und Asset Backed Securities—Grundlagen Praxis Bewertung. Verlag Dr. Müller, Saarbrücken

Miller A (2007) Trade services—pooled payables securitisation. http://www.gtreview.com/news/global/trade-services-pooled-payables-securitisation/

Moller S (2000) Securitisation—a safe bet for your assets. The Treasurer 2000 (March). http://www.treasurers.org/ACTmedia/Sept00TTMoller40-2.pdf

Nassr I, Wehninger G (2015) Unlocking SME finance through market-based debt: securitisation, private placements and bonds. Financial Market Trends 2014(2):89–189

Pfaue M (2003) Strukturierte finanzierung—asset backed strukturen. Schäffer-Poeschel, Stuttgart

PwC (2015) Securitisation in Luxembourg. https://www.pwc.lu/en/securitisation/docs/pwc-securitisation.pdf

Rutan E, Bate S, Bushweller S (2003) The fundamentals of asset-Backed commercial paper. http://www.imf.org/external/np/seminars/eng/2010/mcm/pdf/rutan1.pdf

Schlitt M (2014) Finanzierungsstrategien im Mittelstand. Springer Gabler, Wiesbaden

Chapter 4
Background III—What Is Blockchain Technology?

4.1 Defining the Blockchain and Its Key Technical Aspects

The original blockchain concept described by the inventor of Bitcoin, Satoshi Nakamoto, has undergone various improvements with the objective of overcoming certain issues and rendering the technology more scalable and less hostile to regulators. This chapter presents the principal technical aspects of the Bitcoin blockchain and the most relevant improvements to other projects. We will then look at other more general terms,[1] such as 'distributed ledger technology' (DLT) or 'crypto technologies', which refers to all technologies that can transfer and/or store data using a group consensus protocol on distributed database systems. The terms 'distributed ledger technology' and 'blockchain' are used interchangeably, as the terminology is still evolving.

4.1.1 Peer-to-Peer Value Exchange System

Bitcoin provided the answer to a growing need for a payment system that could adapt to the new way of communications—a coin that is fast, secure and borderless (Antonopoulos 2014). However, the emergence of a full viable digital money—or any digital asset such as stocks, bonds or licenses—presents two principal technical issues: the confirmation of authenticity and the double-spending problem.

Unlike physical assets, digital cash or other digital assets are simply a computer file (sequence of bits), and just like any other digital file, they can be copied. If there

---

[1]Terminology is still evolving and strict definitions have not yet been fully established (IFF 2015).

© The Author(s) 2018
E. Hofmann et al., *Supply Chain Finance and Blockchain Technology*,
SpringerBriefs in Finance, DOI 10.1007/978-3-319-62371-9_4

are no intermediaries who keep a ledger of the account holder's balances (such as cash or securities account balances), one could simply send the file and retain a copy of it. This is known as the double-spending problem, and to prevent it, each note must be checked online against a central ledger when spent (Cham 1992). An authoritative record of all transactions of the digital asset is therefore needed.

The solution proposed by Nakamoto to prevent these two problems relies on a constantly updated and publicly distributed ledger system combined with public or private key cryptography and a particular consensus mechanism.

> We propose a solution to the double-spending problem using a **peer-to-peer** distributed **timestamp server** to generate computational proof of the chronological order of transactions (Nakamoto 2009, p. 8).

Schollmeier (2002) defines a peer-to-peer network as a distributed network architecture (Fig. 4.1), where the participants share a part of their own hardware resources, such as processing power or storage capacity. These shared resources are necessary to provide the service and content offered by the network (e.g. file sharing, storing or shared workspaces for collaboration), and they are directly accessible by other peers without passing by intermediary entities. Contrary to the current banking system, Bitcoin transactions, for instance, are broadcast, recorded and stored by the many participants of the network and not in any central proprietary server, which allows transactions to be finalised in minutes because no reconciliation or any manual intervention is needed in the background.

As mentioned by Dykes (1995), before digital cash can gain wide acceptance, it must gain and keep the public trust. For this reason, counterfeiting must be prevented at all costs. As digital currency is merely bits that represent value, digital currency transactions have to be carried out in such a way as to prevent tampering in transit, on receipt or in storage (Dykes 1995). This authoritative record is the blockchain, a shared database where all transactions are registered in blocks by an

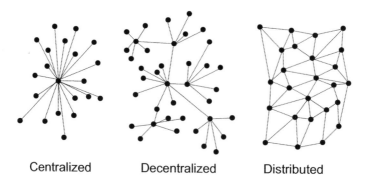

Centralized   Decentralized   Distributed

Fig. 4.1 Graphical representation of centralised to distributed systems (adapted from Swanson 2015)

architecturally distributed peer-to-peer network. By 'timestamp server', it is meant that all transactions are 'time-stamped'[2] in order to prove that the data must have existed at a given time and to give a chronological order to the blocks of trans-actions. Each new block is then cryptographically chained with the one before, reinforcing the whole history of transactions. The history of all transactions defines the owners of the coins, creating de facto unique assets (digital tokens) that are impossible to copy. In the case of cryptocurrencies like Bitcoin, in fact, it is the-oretically impossible for a malicious participant to redo part of the history (i.e. the chain of digital blocks in which the transaction was registered) after a certain coin had been spent in order to cancel the transaction and thus spend the same coin twice (Nakamoto 2009).

The solution to preventing tampering is instead offered by digital signatures, a concept first proposed in 1976 by W. Diffie and M. Hellman that Nakamoto inte-grated into his blockchain design. A digital signature transforms the message (i.e. the transaction) into a cryptographically signed file so that anyone who reads it can be sure of who sent it. The signatures employ a secret key used to sign messages and a public key used to verify them so that only messages signed with the private key can be verified by means of the public one (see **Excursus A**). This process is known as cryptographic proof, and the electronic coins are defined as a chain of digital signatures (Chaum 1992). The possession of the keys to unlock the coins is, therefore, the equivalent to the possession of cash, and if the private key is lost, all the coins contained in the corresponding digital wallet are lost too (Antonopoulos 2014, p. 231).

The Bitcoin blockchain protocol is schematically illustrated in Fig. 4.2.

Excursus A—Public or private key cryptography
Hash functions take a message as input and produce an output that is referred to as a hash code, or simply a hash. Whatever data is put into one of these functions (a string), they return a random number of the same bit size so that it is impossible to predict what they will return given a certain input. Furthermore, the hash is a one-way function, and it cannot be decrypted back, offering security against tampering. The basic idea of cryptographic hash functions is that a hash value serves as a compact representative image (sometimes called an imprint, digital fingerprint or message digest) of an input string, and it can be used as if it were uniquely identifiable with that string (Menezes et al. 1995).

---

[2]The timestamp is a 4-byte file, which is based on the number of seconds elapsed from 1 January 1970, midnight UTC/GMT (Epoch Unit Timestamp) (Antonopoulos 2014, p. 188). At the time of writing (2 March 2016, 11:59 A.M), the time is 1456916388 (http://www.epochconverter.com/).

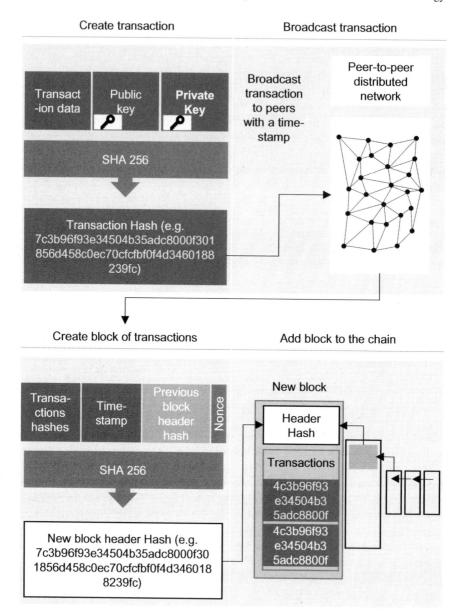

Fig. 4.2 The (Bitcoin) blockchain protocol

Here is an example[3] with the SHA256 hash function used by Bitcoin—the hash of the input 'I like Tuscan wine' is:

7c3b96f93e34504b35adc8000f301856d458c0ec70cfcfbf0f4d3460188239fc

If that string is changed by just one character, the function will get something completely different—here is the hash of 'I like Turcan wine':

f9cbd8bbef04d5b429487becdb9d6601123c8c1d34d47f51f348a38319a430d4

Example of a cryptographic proof[4]:

To spend a digital coin, one has to prove to be the true owner of a public key address from where money is sent. The message and the private key (input) are a sequence of 'n' bits that are hashed through the cryptographic hash function (f) previously described. The output is the generated signature:

$$signature = f\,(message, private\,key)$$

The receiver of the message can then verify through the mathematical algorithmic function (v) behind the signature and the public key of the sender if the transaction actually corresponds to the private key:

$$1 = v\,(message, public\,key, signature)$$

In this example, if the mathematical function returns a value of '1', then the sender is the true owner of the public key. This technique avoids the possibility of fraud while maintaining the privacy of those who use it.

Contrary to the actual centralised systems that rule the mainstream economy, the distributed ledger approach pushes the responsibility and control to the wide network through the proof of work hash-based processes and, more importantly, to the single users. As stated before, private keys are the only proof of ownership for the digital assets, and securing the private keys is therefore a central issue, because if hacked, the entire content of the digital wallet is lost. This is because in the blockchain database there is no personal data stored anywhere, and the transactions are anonymous. While with digital money it could be possible to hedge the problem by storing digital cash in different wallets, the issue becomes more critical if property titles or security interests are registered on the blockchain, too. Property titles and security interests are in fact much more valuable and non-divisible; thus, few jurisdictions would probably allow the registration of property titles on it (Sams 2015). Moreover, if a number of

---

[3]Calculated with the SHA256 hash calculator, from http://www.xorbin.com/tools/sha256-hash-calculator.

[4]Due to the complexity of the cryptographic proof protocol, the example is simplified. The purpose is to show the underlying process behind cryptographic proof.

specialised startups are offering private key security services or the possibility of offline storage in 'cold-wallets' in the near future, appropriately securing private keys becomes a priority preceding mass adoption.

4.1.2 Group Consensus Mechanism

A blockchain-enabled, decentralised accounting system poses the problem of maintaining a single global truth between the different actors of the network who store the transaction's history. In order to permit the nodes to reach a consensus on the actual status of the ledger, an unequivocal group consensus mechanism is needed. The Bitcoin blockchain uses the proof-of-work (PoW) consensus mechanism (see **Excursus B**). This mechanism consists of solving a hard computational problem (a hash problem) at the time of creating new blocks of transactions. The consensus protocol is based on a problem that is difficult to solve but easy to verify, thus avoiding the possibility other nodes could redo the whole PoW in order to accept the transactions. Through this mechanism, every block is linked with the previous one, forming a chain.

Excursus B—The proof-of-work (PoW) consensus mechanism
A decentralised accounting system poses the problem of maintaining a single global truth between the different actors of the network. Following the principles of the hashing functions, the idea is to insert the timestamp (e.g. 1456916388) into the inputs with the hash of all transactions—the merkle root[5]–with the header hash of the previous block and an arbitrary number called 'nonce' (Nakamoto 2009). The blocks are said to be 'chain-linked', because the hash function contains the header hash of the previous block (see Fig. 5.8). Except for the nonce, all the other inputs are given. The problem to solve is now to find the right nonce that produces an output hash (the new header hash) with a value that begins with a large number of zeros. Finding a hash that begins with a given number of zeros is a hard computational task, and the only way to solve this problem is through iteration (Antonopoulos 2014, p. 194)—the computer is asked to run billions and billions of hash computations until it solves the problem.[6] This calculated nonce is the 'proof of work', and the work performed to find it is called mining (Fig. 4.3).

---

[5]The merkel root is constructed by recursively hashing pairs of nodes of the merkel tree until there is only one hash. Merkel trees are the summary of all transactions and provide an efficient process to verify whether a transaction is included in a block (Antonopoulos 2014, p. 164).

[6]For Bitcoin, it takes on average 150 quadrillion hash calculations per second for the network to solve the problem, which means a block every 10 min (Antonopoulos 2014, p. 194).

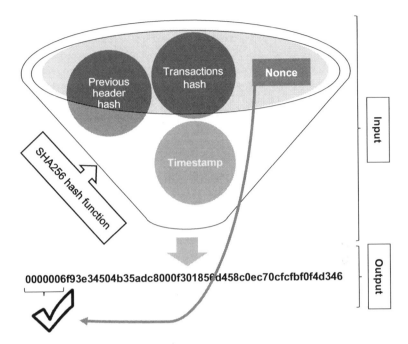

Fig. 4.3 Generation of an SHA256 'time-stamped' block header hash

Whenever a node solves the hash problem, it broadcasts the candidate block along with the proof of work to the other nodes so they can verify it by inserting the broadcast nonce into the hash function. If for the majority the output begins with the same number of zeros, the block is accepted, and nodes start hashing on top of that block, continuing the chain.

With the PoW mechanism, Bitcoin secures the network and the integrity of the transaction database, making the blockchain's history practically immutable after a certain number of blocks. An acceptable level of security is reached after six mined blocks (i.e. one hour) (Antonopoulos 2014, p. 160), whereas newly mined coins can be spent only when the block containing the first transaction—the issuance of the coin—is 100 blocks back (p. 160), which takes 17 h on average.

Since Bitcoin was launched, alternatives to the PoW consensus protocol have emerged, such as script proof of work, multi-algorithm proof of work or hybrid ones, which allow for the acceleration of the block generation time (Antonopoulos 2014, p. 215). BlackCoin (http://blackcoin.co/), for example, uses a different validation process called 'proof-of-stake'. In this system, instead of solving the PoW, the nodes that generate blocks have to provide a proof that they have access to a certain amount of coins before being accepted by the network. This alternative validation process reduces the expected block time down to less than one minute (Vasin n.a).

The debate as to which validation process can best simultaneously guarantee speed, efficiency and security seems unresolved, but PoW appears to be the most commonly used process (Antonopolous 2014). With the actual block size being limited to 1 MB, old and new estimates place the theoretical maximum at 7 transactions per second (bitcoin.it), which unfortunately is not sufficient to serve the mainstream economy. In comparison, Visa's network can process more than 1000 transactions per second, and in an official release in 2013, Nasdaq claimed to be capable of more than 1 million transactions per second in a trading day.

4.1.3 Private and Public Distributed Validation Networks

Even today, the permission-less public blockchain requires security measures (PoW) that limit its wider application to more extensive uses. Furthermore, a 2014 study by the National University of Ireland concluded that the energy consumption used to generate the (Bitcoin) blockchain and keep the system running, under reasonable assumptions, is on par with Ireland's entire energy consumption. The study also concluded that the entire 'industry' is theoretically deficient, given that costs of the single miners (i.e. the network participants that update the blockchain) exceed the rewards (O'Dwyer and Malone 2014).

Furthermore, the mining industry is composed of largely unknown parties (large miners), many of whom are ideologically opposed to corporations or are located in countries with weak legal systems (Greeenspan 2015, p. 11). For example, the Bitcoin network is controlled by a large mining pool, such as Bitfury or F2Pool (bitcoin.info) that could potentially control over 51% of the hash calculation power and rewrite the information contained in a recently created block. This possibility could therefore undermine the regulatory requirements of irrevocability and finality of financial transactions required in capital markets (Swanson 2015, p. 23).

For these reasons, various financial institutions have begun to grasp the idea of having their own private networks or joint systems with trusted and preselected validation nodes called permissioned ledgers. This concept, as underlined in a paper released by the Institute of International Finance (IFF) (2015), is clearly in conflict with the fully decentralised design of Bitcoin and of many other cryptocurrencies or alternative service providers, but it is probably still valid for the financial industry.

> Permissioned ledgers may well be more useful because you don't need to do proof of work, so all of a sudden you can have a business model with much higher transaction throughput.
> A. Batlin, Senior Innovation Manager at UBS, 2014

Essentially, instead of having a fully public and uncontrolled network secured by hard computing techniques, such as the PoW, these solutions create a system where access permissions are tightly controlled and where rights to modify or even read the blockchain state are restricted to selected users.

In a 2015 blog article, Buterin identified two categories of permissioned blockchain applications: (1) consortium blockchains and (2) fully private blockchains.

1. *Consortium blockchains* are distributed ledger systems where the consensus process is controlled by a preselected set of nodes. For example, a consortium of 15 financial institutions, each of which operates a node and of which 10 must sign every block in order for the block to be valid. The right to read the blockchain may be public or restricted to the participants.
2. In *fully private blockchains*, permissions remain centralised to one organisation, and read permissions may be public or restricted to a closed number of participants. Likely applications include database management, auditing or other internal uses for a single company, so public readability may not be necessary in many cases at all.

Permissioned blockchains have the advantage of hard computational block creation not being necessary, as the validation nodes are known (Greenspan 2015). This allows faster validation processes and increased scalability, and they are therefore more adaptable to the transaction volumes of the mainstream economy and would be more favourable to regulators and legislators (IFF 2015).

4.1.4 Smart Contracts

Smart contract is an event-driven program which runs on a replicated shared ledger and which can take custody over assets on that ledger. R. Brown, CTO at R3 CEV

One of the major innovators in the blockchain space is the Ethereum project. The kernel of its principles was first proposed in 2013 in a white paper written by one of its inventors, V. Buterin. Ethereum is an open source BCT with a built-in Turing-complete programming language (Buterin 2013). The Turing-completeness programming language allows anyone to create and write code, commands and decentralised applications on a blockchain for creating their own arbitrary rules for ownership, transaction formats and state transition functions (Buterin 2013), which basically operate as a small computer program. Digital assets, then, can be directly controlled by a piece of code implementing arbitrary rules, a principle first described in the 1990s by N. Szabo and named 'smart contracts'. For Szabo (1994), smart contracts are a computerised transaction protocol that executes the terms of a contract. The general objectives of smart contract design are to satisfy common contractual conditions (such as payment terms, liens, confidentiality and even enforcement), minimise exceptions both malicious and accidental and minimise the need for trusted intermediaries.

Flood and Goodenough (2015) illustrate how legal rules and the consequent structures of financial contracts could be directly described in computational terms.

They demonstrate that contracts are state transition systems that encode explicit transition rules for shifting the relationship from one state to another. Those states are triggered by the realisation of certain predefined events, such as a performance by the counterparties themselves or the occurrence of particular contingencies that may be within or outside their control (for example 'due date passed', 'good shipped' or '1 m LIBOR rate = 0.45'). Blockchain-driven smart contracts can react with those events (as inputs) and make sure logic is accurately executed (provide an output) across untrusted entities without modification by any one party (and abuse) of the written program (Swanson 2015, p. 15). There are three key elements that distinguish smart contracts from ordinary contracts (Swan 2015, p. 16):

1. *Autonomy*: Once a smart contract is launched and running, it does not need to be in further contact with its initiating agent.
2. *Self-sufficiency*: A smart contract has the ability to independently marshal any kind of resource. For example, a smart contract could raise funds by providing services or issuing equity and could spend them on needed resources, such as processing power storage.
3. *Decentralisation*: Smart contracts are registered into blockchains and are thus distributed and self-executed across a wide network of nodes.

According to Lang (2015), smart contracts can react to external events and could be applied to assets represented outside a blockchain (p. 18). First, the parties establish the conditions, the assets under custody and the obligations, and they register the smart contract on a blockchain. Once the events established under the specified conditions trigger the contract execution, the programming logic automatically dictates the movements of value based on the conditions met. For digital assets on a blockchain (e.g. Bitcoin), the accounts are automatically settled, whereas for digital representation of assets off a blockchain (e.g. securities, stocks), accounts are considered settled when accounts off-chain match the settlement instructions (p. 18). Figure 4.4 illustrates a smart contract set-up and execution flow.

It is not clear whether the input information has to be on the same blockchain of the smart contract or not, because according to Greenspan (2016), the inputs must also be submitted to a consensus process; if not, the network could not agree on a

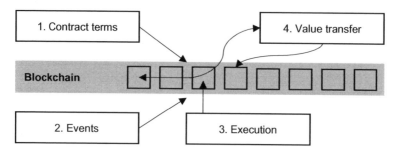

Fig. 4.4 Successive actions in a smart contract set-up and execution (adapted from Swanson 2015, p. 18)

certain output state. Gendal (2015) also agrees that successful smart contract execution relies on the quality of the inputs that are sent to them. Another critical point is given by the weak knowledge of coding languages in the legal frameworks (Flood and Goodenough 2015, p. 30), with the consequence being that it is difficult for jurisdictions to view smart contracts as actual and valid legal contracts (Swanson 2015, p. 16; Gendal 2015).

4.2 A Distributed Ledger's Landscape of Blockchain Technology

As previously mentioned, distributed ledgers can be maintained through a private network of validated nodes or through a shared permission-less public one. Bitcoin—at the time of writing this book—is by far the biggest network, counting more than 4000 nodes (bitcoin.info). The blockchain codes are usually open source, which

Table 4.1 A landscape of distributed ledger approaches

	Traditional centralised database	Fully private DLT	Permissioned consortium DLT	Permission-less public DLT
Network	Many private networks (intranet VPN), silo systems	Private (intranet)	Private validation/public ledger (intranet)	Public (Internet)
Protocol	EDI, HTTP	Any open source protocol, modified or own protocol	Any open source protocol, modified or own protocol	Open source protocols (e.g. Bitcoin, Ethereum)
Validation mechanism	Manual, singularly automated by internal protocols	Organised between participant nodes (e.g. Ripple's BPCA)	Organised between participant nodes. Low difficulty PoW or PoS for integrity	Through PoW, PoS
Scripting system	Turing-complete	Turing-complete or limited script	Turing-complete or limited script	Turing-complete (e.g. Ethereum) or limited script (e.g. Bitcoin)
Security	Central organised identity system and private and costly data storage	Decentral organised identity system (nodes are known and legally prosecutable)	Decentral organised identity system (nodes are known and legally prosecutable) or PoW, PoS	Through PoW or PoS difficulty and crypto-economic theory
Privacy	Confidentiality of centrally stored data	Organised between participant	Through cryptography	Through cryptography

means that groups of developers can work by maintaining and enhancing the software or innovating it with complementary products, services or applications. Since open source software can be used for commercial purposes (opensource.org 2016), a very large number of successful crypto-projects use the open source code protocol of the three major shared ledger providers with the highest market capitalisation[7] (like Bitcoin, Ethereum and Ripple). Table 4.1 illustrates a simplified database systems landscape.

4.3 Key Features of Blockchain Technology

The blockchain was originally designed to transfer value only in the form of digital currencies, and its transaction logic implements a token system that is designed to simply transfer balances from one party to another (Dermody 2015). This means that the maximum complexity of the transaction logic of the network in question is limited to the recording of balances in digital assets along with simple multi-signature authentication. Systems integrating digital assets within the Bitcoin blockchain can use coloured coin (an open source protocol) to encode asset issuance and transfer it as a crypto coin (en.bitcoin.it). The Bitcoin blockchain can be used as a secure, public, append-only store that timestamps and cryptographically signs hashes, which represent a transaction of assets or a document, and validates the ownership of assets and the validity of documents. This occurs without using escrow services, notaries or any trusted third party and allows a high level of 'straight through processing' (STP).

With Turing-complete blockchains (e.g. Ethereum), the technology now has the capability of implementing a broader range of software routines, including the entirety of what is offered by mere token systems, which opens up the possibility of also representing financial securities and instruments (e.g. smart-bonds) directly on the distributed ledger without reference to central databases and all of their associated disadvantages (Dermody 2015).

Lewis (2015) identifies two uses for blockchains and DLT: the digital token and activities registries.

- A *digital token* is the representation of an asset (e.g. coins, bonds or stocks) for which ownership is tracked on a blockchain, since transactions are registered and validated by the network (e.g. private or public).

---

[7]For the complete list see on http://coinmarketcap.com/all/views/all/.

- *Activities registries* are instead used to securely store data, usually under the form of hashes, which are a sort of 'fingerprint' of standardised information (e.g. trade facts or identity information). The hashes on the blockchain prove that given facts existed at a time-stamped time and that the parties who signed them agreed on these facts.

In order to evaluate the possible applications, we list the key features derived from the technical aspects analysed in the previous sections. The capacity of a blockchain (1) to act as a notary, (2) perform the clearing and settlement of transactions, (3) automate contractual relations, (4) provide an immutable (public) data storage facility and (5) provide transparent real-time data.

1. *Notarisation*

Because of the time-stamped hash-based algorithm that 'governs' the distributed ledger, all information registered in it is automatically authenticated and time-stamped without the need for an intermediary (e.g. a notary). Interested parties can know with certainty that given information existed at a particular date and time. The possibility of hashing documents in a blockchain guarantees authenticity and prevents potential tampering.

2. *Clearing and settlement*

Potentially, a blockchain allows transfers of any kind of digital asset or asset representation without the need for trusted third parties through private/public key encryption and efficient settlement of transactions and processing using the distributed ledger. Cash or securities are settled in near real time, since the trade is complete when the next update to the blockchain is validated. This would remove the need for post-trade affirmation or confirmation and central clearing during the settlement cycle, and it reduces the scope for data errors, disputes and reconciliation lags, which speeds up the end-to-end process (Oliver Wyman and Euroclear 2016, p. 7).

3. *Trusted automation of contractual relations* (e.g. *smart contracts*)

As seen, smart contracts allow for the automation of contractual relations and change the state of assets on a distributed ledger. This concept has fostered the idea of 'smart-bonds', which are securities that have the capacity to execute corporate actions and cash events automatically (interest payments, the redemption of the nominal amount at maturity, splits, knock out events, etc.).[8] The possibility for programs to receive external inputs on a blockchain suggests that external events (e.g. goods received) could alter a state transition of a given digital asset (e.g. IF good received THEN send 20,000 USD to Supplier ELSE back) and therefore reduce or eliminate counterparty risk in trading relationships.

---

[8]UBS revealed in a further report that it is experimenting with smart bond applications using a private fork of Ethereum (Coindesk.com).

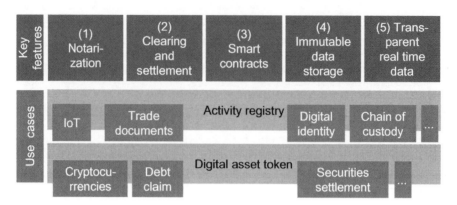

Fig. 4.5 Blockchain's key features use case enablers

4. *Immutable data storage*

Time-stamping transactions, documents or any kind of asset in an ongoing digital chain stored in the network provide an immutable data storage capacity. Data is distributed among participants, and no single actor could remove them. An immutable transactions history could also provide a chain of possession in supply chains, providing a clear indication of provenance and allowing tracking of the traded products (i.e. chain of possession).

5. *Transparent real-time data*

According to a recent working paper by Oliver Wyman and Euroclear (2016), the major benefits of this technology in the financial space are derived from the ability of this technology to provide transparent real-time data. This peculiarity of the blockchain could eliminate the need for data enrichment (such as aligning trade data with settlement data), reconciliations and disputes amongst counterparties (p. 7). Participants could selectively reveal trusted data to another counterparty ahead of trading time to provide greater certainty of their own worthiness and thereby reduce risk and/or credit exposures.

All the presented key features of BCT open up the potential for different use cases, such as those identified by Lewis (2015) and now singularly discussed in Chap. 5 (Fig. 4.5).

References

Antonopoulos MA (2014) Mastering Bitcoin—unlocking digital currencies. O'Reilly, Sebastopol
Buterin V (2013) A next generation smart contract and decentralized application platform. https://ethereumbuilders.gitbooks.io/guide/content/en/whitepaper.html
Cham D (1992) Achieving electronic privacy. Sci Am 267(2):96–101

Dykes JM (1995) Digital cash and the development of the apolitical currency. Ethics and Law on the Electronic Frontier Fall

Dermody R (2015) Smart contract versus "token"-based systems. http://symbiont.io/uncategorized/smart-contract-vs-token-based-systems/

Flood N, Goodenough O (2015) Contracts as automaton: the computational representation of financial agreement. https://financialresearch.gov/working-papers/files/OFRwp-2015-04_Contract-as-Automaton-The-Computational-Representation-of-Financial-Agreements.pdf

Greenspan A (2016) Why many smart contract use cases are simply impossible. http://www.coindesk.com/three-smart-contract-misconceptions/

Gendal R (2015) A simple model for smart contract. https://gendal.me/page/2/

Greenspan G (2015) Ending the bitcoin versus Blockchain debate. http://www.multichain.com/blog/2015/07/bitcoin-vs-Blockchain-debate/

IFF (Institute of International Finance) (2015) The internet of finance: unleashing the potential of Blockchain technology. https://www.iif.com/sites/default/files/general/cmm_rn_20150416.pdf

Lang J (2015). In: Swanson T (Ed) Consensus as a service: a brief report of permissioned, distributed ledger systems. http://www.ofnumbers.com/wp-content/uploads/2015/04/Permissioned-distributed-ledgers.pdf

Lewis A (2015) The emergence of blockchains as activity registers. https://bitsonblocks.net/2016/08/05/the-emergence-of-blockchains-as-activity-registers/

Menezes AJ, Oorschot PC, Vanstone SA (1995) A handbook for applied cryptography. http://citeseer.ist.psu.edu/viewdoc/download?doi=10.1.1.99.2838&rep=rep1&type=pdf

Nakamoto S (2009) A peer-to-peer electronic cash system. https://bitcoin.org/bitcoin.pdf

O'Dwyer KJ, Malone D (2014) Bitcoin mining and its energy footprint. https://karlodwyer.github.io/publications/pdf/bitcoin_KJOD_2014.pdf

Oliver Wyman and Euroclear (2016) Blockchain in capital markets—the prize and the journey. http://www.oliverwyman.com/content/dam/oliver-wyman/global/en/2016/feb/Blockchain-In-Capital-Markets.pdf

opensource.org (2016) The open source definition. https://opensource.org/osd-annotated

Sams R (2015) Bitcoin blockchain for distributed clearing: a critical assessment. J Financial Trans 42:39–46

Schollmeier R (2002) A definition of peer-to-peer networking for the classification of peer-to-peer architectures and applications. Paper presented at the first international conference on peer-to-peer computing, Linkoping University, Sweden, 27–29 August 2001

Swan E (2015) Blockchain: Blueprint for a New Economy. O'Reilly, Sebastpol

Swanson T (2015) Consensus as a service: a brief report of permissioned, distributed ledger systems. http://www.ofnumbers.com/wp-content/uploads/2015/04/Permissioned-distributed-ledgers.pdf

Szabo N (1994) Smart contracts. http://szabo.best.vwh.net/smart.contracts.html

Vasin P (no date) BlackCoin's proof-of-stake protocol. http://blackcoin.co/blackcoin-pos-protocol-v2-whitepaper.pdf

Chapter 5
Concept—Where Are the Opportunities of Blockchain-Driven Supply Chain Finance?

Blockchain is an elegant solution to clean up a tangled mess of documents, databases, regulatory compliance, international boundaries, auditing and management. N. Bauerle, Blockchain strategist and author of the Coindesk.com Report, 2016

As seen in the first chapters, technology plays a central role in supply chain finance (SCF): the improvement of software and platforms allows businesses to come together and speed up process flows throughout the supply chain, enabling various forms of financing solutions—from dynamic discounting via reverse factoring to the more complex reverse securitisation. Nevertheless, some barriers and pain points, which increase the set-up and transaction costs, still exist and have a negative impact on spreads and the value created for the supply chain community and its investors.

Chapter 4 showed how Blockchain technology (BCT) could enable the creation of new services and application programming interfaces (APIs) that promise to lean up structures, speed up processes and make services more efficient and less costly. In order to outline the opportunities, this chapter deals first with the use cases that could help overcome barriers that arise when discussing and presenting the different SCF models, and it then successively analyses the impact of the adoption of this technology by the supply chain communities.

5.1 Dealing with Supply Chain Finance Barriers and Supply Chain Processes

A number of issues have already been described, from questions relating to the accounting treatment of SCF transactions, compliance obligations and the high transaction costs in reverse factoring instruments. The following sections describe the different use cases with related scenarios and identify the opportunities for approved payables financing solutions.

E. Hofmann et al., *Supply Chain Finance and Blockchain Technology*, SpringerBriefs in Finance, DOI 10.1007/978-3-319-62371-9_5

5.1.1 Compliance Requirements (KYC)

BCT as an identity register is a discussed use case for KYC and anti-money laundering (AML) purposes, and such uses fall under the asset registry use cases underlined in Sect. 4.3. The key feature of a decentralized database in which information is immutably recorded and available in near real time would allow other financial entities to access secure and trusted sources of information about new customers, such as IDs, bank related data and any required background documentation. As the onboarding of suppliers onto SCF platforms is manual and complex, usually only the 'top slice' (i.e. the largest suppliers) is invited, and the potential value in the 'long tail' supplier base is lost. A cost-effective KYC check could simplify the suppliers' onboarding process and could allow banks to also include the long-tail supplier-base, supplying funding to a sector (usually smaller SME suppliers) where credit capacity remains limited (Nassr and Wehninger 2015).

Deloitte (2016) sees the technology as particularly useful for this purpose. Their publication underlines how it could be possible to avoid duplication of KYC checks by sharing proper checks and registering them on a Blockchain so that other banks would no longer have to perform the same checks, since adequate evidence will exist on it. Historical records will provide proof that the bank that performed the KYC has done it properly. Other advantages highlighted in this study are that the encrypted details could be updated in near real time so that all banks engaged with a particular customer are updated on the actual status. Once registered on the Blockchain, no single entity could tamper with the historical data, providing a trusted public registry for which access to information could be restricted only to interested parties.

Martinelli and Smith (2015) also underline the significant benefits that a distributed ledger system could bring in handling and organising identity for KYC requirements. They see BCT working as an identity and financial information registrar with banks acting as validators in order to obtain a secure online data source for any other financial provider who needs to comply with KYC requirements for a given client.

Biella and Zinetti (2016) instead propose both a conservative and a disruptive scenario for Blockchain-driven identity management solutions. In the conservative scenario, every bank group will maintain its registry for which they perform the checks, and the information will then be available only for the bank's group entities. According to this solution, each customer will have only a single cryptographic identity so as to avoid any duplicative efforts for customers involved in multiple legal entities and jurisdictions. In the disruptive scenario, any institution could instead issue clients fingerprints (hashes) on the Blockchain, and customer identity will be cryptographically and digitally registered so that the banks that will receive a digital document version from their customers will use the Blockchain registry to prove its authenticity and validity without the need for further due diligence (p. 14). This will drastically speed up the KYC process and thus reduce the compliance costs.

Despite advantages associated with the possibility of reducing (or avoiding) the duplication effort, Goldman Sachs (2016) assume only modest cost savings related to customer onboarding (pp. 74–77). They point out that 'Blockchain would not remove banks' KYC liability, and thus we think banks will remain cautious when onboarding new accounts given AML penalties, despite improvements in customer data transparency and security' (p. 75). They estimate that Blockchain use would decrease customer onboarding headcount by only 10%. This is because banks would still need to run customer diligence checks when the prospective account is a private company or an individual setting up a bank relation for the first time (p. 75). The authors point out that pre-existing customer data on a Blockchain could in fact be questionable if validated by only a single source.

In order to work properly and efficiently, this kind of database will therefore have to achieve a critical mass of participants and validators. Another issue is caused by limitations related to privacy due to confidentiality requirements varying across different legal frameworks (Biella and Zinetti 2016, p. 14).

A cost-effective onboarding process could thus simplify the set-up of SCF programmes, particularly for buyers with a dispersed geographical (from various jurisdictions) supplier-base. Multi-bank SCF solutions could be particularly beneficial, because they can avoid the duplicative effort of the checks, since each bank has to perform them independently. A shared and trusted KYC registry could encourage banks to participate in SCF programmes, increasing competition and thus providing better financing rates.

For reverse securitisation programmes, the advantage will be of a lower magnitude, because KYC requirements for Luxembourg special purpose vehicle companies (SPVs) are already less extensive than for banks (see Chap. 3), but they will also benefit from a simplified compliance process.[1]

5.1.2 Accounting Rules and Treatments

As underlined in Chap. 2, reconciliation from trade payables with bank debts stems from various agreements between the financing provider and the buyer leading the programme. The point is to determine how a Blockchain could avoid reclassification while being in an agreement. The options are to either change the accounting rules or change the way auditors treat the issue. As already discussed, BCT can change the way transactions are processed and the way data is stored and shared, but it cannot change the accounting rules. For this reason, we now discuss whether the technology could have an impact on the way auditors respond to accounting issues.

---

[1]In practice, however, some bank typical KYC requirements need also be applied to SPVs because some bank's compliance rules might demand the same diligence for the SPV's KYC process as if performed by the bank itself.

A list of criteria that is important in keeping approved payables financing as trade debt is presented by Gustin (2014):

- Buyer should not indicate a higher commitment to pay to the financial institution by confirming to the latter that he will pay the invoice at maturity regardless of trade disputes or other rights there may be against the supplier.
- Buyer should always pay on the maturity date stated on the invoice (i.e. no early payments with discounts shared with the bank and no prolonged payment terms with interest payments to the bank).
- There should be no agreement made between the buyer and the bank ('kick-backs') in order to share revenues from the spreads in the form of different kinds of fees for services provided.

As it was originally intended to serve a distributed accounting system for digital cash, Blockchain and distributed ledger technology (DLT) are discussed as uses for corporate accounting. The capacity of Blockchain technology to avoid siloed-systems and reconciliation in corporate accounting could enable a new way of managing ledger entries in a network of companies. A strong focus is set on the potential of changing the auditing processes, based on both a disruptive scenario and more conservative one.

In a disruptive scenario, key features of immutability and transparent real-time data could potentially replace auditors if all business transactions take place on a Blockchain (Lazanis 2015). Since what is registered and validated on it can be trusted, performing an audit would no longer make sense, which would automate and potentially eliminate related audit costs.

A more conservative scenario is presented by Deloitte (2016) that sees the technology features as allowing auditors to automatically verify large portions of the most important data behind the financial statements. The cost and time necessary to conduct an audit will therefore be considerably reduced, and auditors could 'spend freed up time on areas they can add more value, e.g. on very complex transactions or on internal control mechanisms' (p. 3).

As a matter of debate even between auditors in the same office (Gustin 2014), the bank debt versus payable issue could therefore attract more attention due to the freed-up time provided to auditors. The application of BCT in corporate accounting could therefore represent a threat more so than an opportunity. Later in the chapter, this use case will instead be discussed from a different angle for which a number of possible opportunities may arise.

5.1.3 Issuing and Post-trade Clearing and Settlement Processing

Because the financing is provided through securities issuance in the primary market, only reverse securitisation financing would benefit from this specific use. As underlined in Chap. 3, clearing and settlement are fundamental processes that

require various intermediaries, the principal tasks of which rely on matching the
buyer and seller records, confirming that the counterparts agree to the terms and
fulfilling the delivery requirements by exchanging securities against cash (i.e. the
role of a trusted third party). The process requires data reconciliation and manual
intervention because of the multiple ledgers that must be updated, consequently
making post-trade processing slow and costly (actual standards see securities settlement in two to three business days after trade).

Blockchain solutions allow digital securities to be issued directly to the distributed ledger (ESMA 2016, p. 11; Wyman and Euroclear 2016, p. 10).[2]

The asset ledger will store ownership details and transaction history—assuming
the role of custodians (Wyman and Euroclear 2016, p. 11) and smart contracts—
which would sit on top of the ledgers and reduce the uncertainty and counterparty
risk related to contract terms and enhance the automation of the processing (ESMA
2016, p. 10). Distributed ledger technologies could also facilitate the implementation of a unique reference system across securities markets—a unique security
identifier that would be embedded in the system (p. 10). A Blockchain solution
avoids the need of central securities depositories (CSDs) and custodian banks to
manage the process of issuance, clearing and settlement or redemption, which,
according to the market, costs up to 500 EUR for each issuance. Furthermore, with
DLTs, a digital asset (i.e. a single token that represents a security) is settled in near
real-time $(T + 0)$, since the trade is complete when the next update to the
Blockchain is validated by the network (for example, this takes an average of
10 min for the Bitcoin Blockchain and mere milli seconds in the SETL
Blockchain). Since money is tied up until settlement with the actual standards, near
real-time settlement would unlock capital for suppliers and market investors. Since
the funds are released to the suppliers once the note is successfully settled to the
investors, the supplier community will have access to the funds earlier (3 days
represent 10% of a 30 day maturity invoice), leading to lower financing costs. In
addition, the interest period becomes extended by 2 days with the effect that more
payables become eligible for the program, and short-term securities become more
attractive to the investor because they carry a higher interest.

Regulation and legal admission of fiat currency in a Blockchain represents a key
point in order to maintain the promises of faster and cheaper clearing and settlement. According to Mainelli and Milne (2016), the fastest settlement $(T + 0)$
provided by distributed ledger technologies would require pre-disposition of cash
ownership prior to trade and would represent a barrier to adoption due to the change
required at the business process level (p. 14). However, this would probably not be
true if assets, cash and securities were all available on the Blockchain so that
pre-disposition would not be required due to real-time delivery versus payment
(DvP) settlements. Furthermore, switching the ultimate record of ownership from
CSDs and custodians onto a DLT will have to deal with a set of problems

---

[2]Various private or consortium projects such as the Corda R3, Nasdaq Linq, Digital Asset Holding
or SETL.io are addressing this specific financial application.

concerning trust and legality. Today, the vast majority of resources employed in clearing and settlement are in fact required for three other tasks beside the sole transfer of ownership against payment (Mainelli and Milne 2016): (a) establishing trust before final settlement and ensuring that the trade is agreed accurately on both sides and that counterparties are ready and willing to settle; (b) ensuring the legal validity of the exchange; (c) dealing with the exceptions that arise when trust and legal validity are not established automatically through the automated clearing processes carried out before final settlement (p. 24).

But as seen in Chap. 4, counterparties do not need to have established any trust relationship when a transaction is executed on a Blockchain. So with a Blockchain-enabled real-time delivery versus payment (DvP), all these tasks could be handled by the technology itself. Furthermore, cancellation would become easier if real-time settlement is possible, because a quick (real-time) cancellation reduces the risk of losses due to price changes, for example.

McKinsey (2015) and GBST (2016) analysed the possible evolution and scenarios for DLT applications in the capital markets. Both see the adoption of this technology in four different scenarios, which depend on the level of adoption by the capital market participants and the ultimate potential in delivering a peer-to-peer marketplace between issuers and investors. GBST (2016) focuses particularly on the change in the role of custodians and CSDs and the effects on back-office infrastructure for financial providers.

The following are four possible scenarios and their consequent impact on approved payables financing.

Scenario 1—Single adoption
Technology will be adopted directly by CSDs and custodians for specific instrument types (e.g. fixed income) with no significant change in infrastructure (traditional third parties will remain). The technology will enhance the efficiency of the processes, but T + 0 settlement is unlikely to become standard, and the scope of the solution would be limited to secondary low volume market. For issuers, service providers and investors, this scenario provides only minimal cost reductions, and as the notes are issued in the primary market, the reverse securitisation model illustrated in Chap. 3 would not be affected.

Scenario 2—Smart contract enables small subset adoption
Smart contract-driven transactions allow automation between banks in addition to depository and transfer functions. The return processes for short-term securities could be performed automatically, and participants could introduce new functionalities on the system on their own terms. Clearing institutions will still exist, but multiple providers could compete to clear transactions or receive a small fee for the temporary supply of liquidity to the settlement process. Enhanced automation and competition would probably lower transaction fees, potentially drive settlement to trade day plus 1 day (T + 1) and provide automatic redemption at maturity date (M). Figure 5.1 illustrates a simplified notes issuing and post-trade processing.

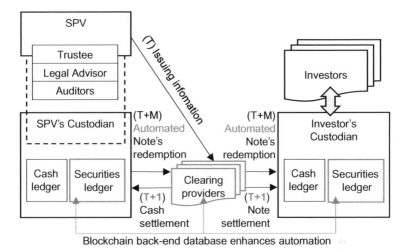

Fig. 5.1 Simplified post-trade clearing and settlement services in the reverse securitisation model (Scenario 2)

Scenario 3—New global infrastructure

Global distributed ledger consortiums would only solve clearing and settlement problems that are currently poorly served by the existing infrastructure, and fixed income post-trade processing would not be the primary focus. Furthermore, it would probably impact international trade, for which CSDs could outsource their function to a globally distributed ledger, while locally the processes would remain unaltered principally due to local market regulations. The reverse securitisation model illustrated in Chap. 3 would not be affected, as fixed income post-trade processing is not seen as the primary focus in this scenario.

Scenario 4—Global peer-to-peer network

Trading and settlement would happen between investors and issuers directly, replacing the traditional capital market system and removing any financial inter-mediary layer between issuer, buyer or seller. Substantially reduced fees due to back-office infrastructure would be replaced by a software that can be installed in the cloud and will provide access to the most commonly required functions. Even if not stated in the report, near real-time settlement should be expected to be the standard in such a disruptive model (Fig. 5.2).

The greatest benefits for capital market investors and corporations exist in Scenario 4, for which third parties' services are not requested or limited. GBST (2016) states that 'several technology platforms capable of providing this service already exist in some form, or are in the process of development' (p. 9).

A general reduction of costs is the main suggested benefit of a DLT application in securities clearing and settlement—particularly by reducing the need for multiple intermediaries—and the capital market community could particularly benefit from

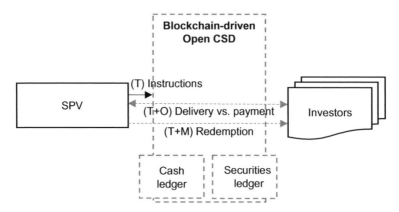

Fig. 5.2 Simplified post-trade clearing and settlement services in the reverse securitisation model (Scenario 4). Adapted from SETL.io (https://www.setl.io/opencsd/#)

reduced transaction costs. A peer-to-peer securities exchange scenario could drastically cut post-trade costs, avoiding the use of existing CSDs and custodians and enabling securities to be settled in near-real time and thus providing funds sooner to suppliers. The London-based financial Blockchain specialist SETL.io has presented the Blockchain-based 'OpenCSD', a platform that combines the trading venues, clearing house and ledgers for issuers and asset owners. Consequently, all functions and services, such as cash management, collateral management, securities lending, corporate actions and reporting, are managed by the 'OpenCSD', making existing CSDs, clearing houses and central counterparty clearing (CCPs) with general clearing members (GCMs) and non-clearing members (NCMs) for cash products obsolete. This would have a far bigger impact than just lower transaction costs, because due to the eliminated settlement risk, GCMs and NCMs would not need to provide collateral to the CCP or clearing fund.

A cost-effective securities settlement process means fewer transaction costs for investors. Especially fixed income securities with short maturities (e.g. SCF reverse securitisations) benefit most from these cost savings as here the costs have the highest proportion compared to the investor's income. The resulting enhanced competition could lower the spreads and potentially allow the onboarding of larger suppliers that have lower marginal fees because of better access to credit conditions. Furthermore, lower transaction costs enable smaller buyer programmes to participate in reverse securitisation programmes, thereby increasing the total market volumes significantly.

From an interview with Nestlé the world's largest food and beverage company it became clear that the issues highlighted in this first part of the chapter capture the attention of world leading companies that benefit from SCF programmes and are concerned with the possible benefits offered by BCT-use cases in this specific area.

Interview with Frédéric Lelieur, Operations controller in charge of Supplier Financing deployment, Nestlé

7th March 2017

Authors Today, Nestlé is running several SCF programmes globally. What was the motivation to offer SCF to your suppliers?

Lelieur *We want to give our suppliers the opportunity to benefit from the capital strength of Nestlé. Simply—and this motivation has not changed since we started SCF—we offer SCF to strengthen the relationship to our suppliers in a context that is mutually beneficial.*

Authors How important is the technology when it comes to supporting the SCF process?

Lelieur *Technology, and in particular the standardization of technology, is one important element when it comes to selecting the right partners. We already experienced banks in the relatively young SCF markets that decided to discontinue their SCF offering virtually overnight. This is an issue for our suppliers. In this case, we need to be quick to replace this partner. By choosing a standardized technology that is easy to adapt and compatible with our processes and technical infrastructure, we mitigate the risk of damaging our supplier relationships or—even more crucial—their financial solvency.*

Authors Where do you see the roadblocks of SCF, and how could Blockchain technology help to overcome these barriers?

Lelieur *Fraud is a risk when deploying SCF, and therefore we carefully monitor the sources of information and the technology that is transporting this information. Here, we believe that the Blockchain technology can play an important role to prevent fraud and provide additional security to the chain of payments. Moreover, Blockchain can cut intermediaries and reduce process steps. Blockchain technology provides the potential that the full transaction flow will be processed in a single technical environment that is secure due to the approval of many entities that share the same distributed ledger. By reducing the number of involved parties and by simplifying the transaction, we also expect that the cost per transaction can be reduced significantly for our suppliers and therefore make the SCF programs more attractive to them. This is important to Nestlé.*

Authors One of the main SCF-related Blockchain use cases is KYC. What is your view as a corporation on the impact of BCT on KYC?

Lilieur   *From the corporation's point of view, we are not directly affected, as our suppliers are existing relationships and thus there is no need for us to KYC them again when they are offered to join an SCF program. Nevertheless, I see the relevance of KYC for SCF programs. It is one of the critical hurdles in the supplier onboarding process for our SCF partners, and it can result in significant costs for the highly regulated banking industry. Therefore, KYC today is one reason why SCF programs may not be available to those smaller and weaker suppliers that could actually benefit the most from the positive effects of SCF, such as early collection and access to lower financing rates. It is Nestlé's ambition to include all types of suppliers, including from countries where KYC is today difficult and costly, because our main motivation for SCF is to strengthen the close collaboration with our suppliers.*

Authors   A wide definition that is often used by experts is 'Blockchain lets you put all of the information across all of the participants so that everyone can do useful things with it while maintaining a single source of truth'. Translated to supply chain finance, it would mean that all invoices appear in a distributed ledger, enriched by SCF relevant information, such as current ownership of a certain receivable (i.e. is it still owned by the supplier or assigned to a factor, is the invoice offered to a supply chain finance program, has it a 'promise-to-pay' from the debtor, etc.). Only those market participants provided with a special key would be able to read only those pieces of information that are relevant to them. Thereby, legal validity and a lot more information that gives transparency and security to the involved parties could be assured by Blockchain technology. What is your take on this scenario—'Common practice in 5–10 years', or rather 'Brave new world'?

Lelieur   *From where we stand, this seems currently hard to believe. In its pure form, it would mean that there is a global distributed ledger that holds all invoices of all market participants, and therefore all past and present invoice information is stored in all Blockchain nodes. I am sceptical whether today this is technical feasible or commercially viable.*

Authors   Compared to putting all relevant invoice information in the Blockchain, money transfers via the Blockchain seem to be a doable use. But does it have a relevance for SCF from the corporation's point of view?

Lelieur   *Yes, but not a very big one. High costs for cross-border payments always have a negative impact on the funding offered to our suppliers, and the reduction in costs for payments would ultimately be beneficial to all parties.*

> Authors Some SCF platforms securitize bundled invoices to finance the
> SCF programme. Due to current settlement standards, it takes about
> 3 days to receive the money after the supplier has elected to sell an
> invoice and collect early. Moreover, the buyer typically must
> transfer the due invoice amount 2 days before the securities
> redemption date. With Blockchain-driven settlements and pay-
> ments, these time lags could be reduced to zero.
>
> Lelieur *Yes, it has a positive effect, but for most suppliers, 3 days are no
> issue. However, for suppliers that use "blind factoring" arrange-
> ments, 3 days might be the decisive reason to participate in an SCF
> programme or not. But a far more crucial area where discounting
> days may be reduced is the buyer's invoice approval time. Here,
> may lose potentially weeks not just days until they can approve an
> invoice. That is a field where the high level of standardization and
> transparency brought through the Blockchain technology may
> prove to be a strong enabler for SCF programmes.*

5.1.4   Relevant Supply Chain Activities

Because dealing only with the capacity to overcome certain barriers could mean neglecting other important opportunities offered by this new technology, this section also takes a different approach. In fact, SCF services could be strongly influenced by the adoption of new technologies or solutions on the corporate side. The automation of B2B processes provided by the development of ERP systems, as well as the rise of e-invoicing, is an important enabler of faster and more efficient SCF solutions. As our focus is on approved payables financing, the procurement and fulfilment processes (Magal and Word 2011)—following the key steps, namely (a) order processing, (b) shipping, (c) billing and invoicing and (d) payment—are of special interest.

(a) *Order processing*

A buyer sends a purchase order (PO)—a commitment to purchase some goods under specific terms and conditions—to his supplier via EDI or web services. This triggers the sales processing steps in the supplier's ERP system with the creation of a sales order. A sales order contains data related to shipping, billing, partner functions and data from the buyer. After this step, a transfer of requirements for the material planning process is generated. Before filling the sales order, an availability check is performed in order to determine whether the material can be shipped as requested.

(b) *Shipping and material flow*

The shipping step takes place once the orders become due for delivery. At this point, a delivery document and a transfer order for warehouse management are created. When the shipment has left the facility, a *post good issued* is generated in the supplier's ERP system, and the sales order is updated with the shipment details. Once the goods are transferred to the buyer, it matches the delivery document with the related PO and creates a good receipt document with the related PO number. A signed bill of lading issued by the carrier accompanies the delivered goods as proof of shipment for Incoterms obligations.

(c) *Billing and invoicing*

After successful shipment,[3] a billing due list is updated, and the billing step can be executed. Billing utilizes the data from the delivery document and the sales order (material number and quantity) and creates an invoice. After receiving the invoice, the buyer verifies it before making the payment. A common method of verification is the three-way-match between PO, goods receipt (or any delivery document) and the invoice. Once approved, the account is debited.

(d) *Payment*

The buyer selects the payment method and bank. Payments could be made automatically with a specific software, which retrieves all authorised invoices within a specified timeframe and automatically generates payments. The cash transfer is not instantaneous, but funds may take several hours or even days to move from the buyer's account to the seller's account, and certain fees are collected. For international wires transfers, the delays and fees are expected to be higher.

5.2 Layers of Blockchain-Driven Supply Chains

From the previous section, it is possible to derive the four layers of interaction between a buyer and a supplier (i.e. a payment, billing, shipping and an order-processing layer) (Fig. 5.3). While ERP systems allow the partial integration of different layers into one wide application system, silos (i.e. isolated operating units and layers) can still exist within the same organization. This leads to reconciliation efforts and manual updates from one system to another with weak integration between the different layers and the risk of human errors.

---

[3]In the case of a new customer or poor payment history, suppliers usually request payment before shipping (Magal and Word 2011, pp. 5–39).

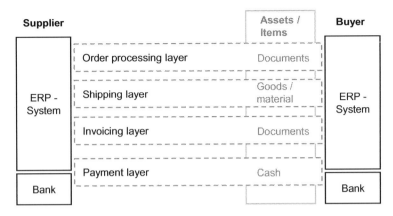

Fig. 5.3 The four supply chain-layers between buyer and supplier

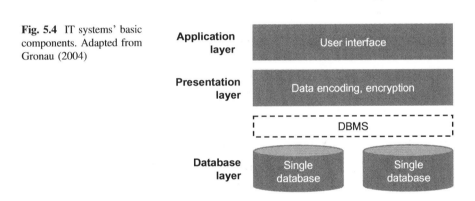

Fig. 5.4 IT systems' basic components. Adapted from Gronau (2004)

An IT system such as an ERP basically consists of three basic components: a database layer, a presentation layer and an application layer (Kent 1987) (Fig. 5.4). The produced data is stored in a single database, which is made available through database management systems (DBMS) (Gronau 2004, p. 9) in which typical data producers are ERP users from the 'front-end' departments, such as sales and purchasing (Röthlin 2010, p. 116). As each organization's ERP is built upon a single database in order to run the ERP's application layer, the assets and items exchanged are transferred from one organization's individual database to another. With the use of Blockchains as underlying technology, all the information is recorded and broadcast across all of the participants so that everyone can use it as a basic component for their applications while maintaining a single source of truth.

5.2.1 The Order Processing Layer

The order-processing workflow starts with a PO from the buyer. Within the Blockchain, once created, the PO is time-stamped and can become a valid document whose clauses can be executed only if valid, due to the programming features of smart contracts (Camerinelli 2016, p. 9). Purchase orders can become 'live' contracts that are always subject to possible adaptations, and changes can be tracked by the embedded time-stamp when key metadata is registered on the Blockchain. Assuming delivery documents can also be registered on it, the metadata of the invoice, PO and bill of lading could be matched automatically due to the smart contracts feature, which ensures consistency between price and quantity in all three documents (i.e. three-way-match), permitting an automated and fast invoice approval. The entire history of the transactions offers perfect audibility, and trust between parties is provided by the immutability of the data entered in a Blockchain.

5.2.2 The Shipping Layer

Keeping track of the material flow at each step, along with the corresponding paper flow, is a major undertaking that requires manual processes that are subject to human error, loss, damage or even theft and fraud (Harris 2016). For example, Provenance—a London-based startup—offers a Blockchain-based application that provides chain of custody along the supply chain for a given product or item. Information is open to end customers to prove the authenticity and provide assurance against counterfeits, and the product can be tracked along the supply chain. Another potential application is provided by smart contracts and cryptographic multi-signatures for all the various documentation and processing stages involved in a trade transaction (EBA 2015, p. 14). For example, a documentary trade could be ruled on a Blockchain, and execution of the payment to a vendor could be automated when certain criteria is met [e.g. goods have been received or shipped or a particular date has been reached, (EBA 2015, p. 14)]. The transfer of title would be secure due to being triggered by a smart contract representing pre-set contractual agreements (Camerinelli 2016, p. 10).

Furthermore, Wave Inc.—an Israeli-based startup—is creating a product that aims to take the place of traditional bills of lading using the Bitcoin Blockchain. It aims to replicate the industry standard workflows but replace printed documents with versions that are stored electronically in Blockchain transaction metadata, managing the ownership of each document or good in transport (Bauerle 2016, p. 13).

Other solutions, such as the IBM's autonomous decentralized peer-to-peer telemetry (ADEPT), propose an even higher integration level by combining internet of things (IoT) with BCTs. Right from the time that a product completes final assembly, it can be registered into a Blockchain representing its beginning of life so that the product remains a unique entity within that Blockchain throughout its life when it passes from owner to owner (IBM 2015, p. 6). In such a Blockchain-based IoT, there is the possibility of maintaining product information, its history, product revisions, warranty details and end of life, transforming the Blockchain into a trusted database. IBM (2015) also postulates the possibility of devices and products that engage in autonomous transactions and form records.

The potential of having all the information written in a Blockchain allows the creation of an authoritative record that can be used to automatically establish smart contracts. Without such an authoritative record, smart contracts written on a Blockchain could hardly be executed, because parties need to agree on data and information that, like smart contracts themselves, are agreed to by a whole network through a consensus mechanism.

The one-layer Blockchain solution sees as such a fully integrated and automated trade network where documents and goods are transparently identified and tracked along the supply chain. Because the information is registered on a distributed database, it makes it tamper-resistant and fosters greater trust in the trade network.

5.2.3 The Invoicing Layer

As explained in Harris (2016) and Lawlor (2016), the principal purpose of 'tokenizing' invoices on a Blockchain is to avoid fraud and double-financing issues in invoice discounting and factoring. Blockchain-based services can register the invoice-related information on a Blockchain in order to avoid duplicates and fraud across the network (Harris 2016). As explained by Lawlor (2016), each invoice would be distributed across the network and, similar to Bitcoin transactions, hashed and time-stamped in order to create a unique identifier. If a supplier tried to sell same invoice again through the network, that invoice would indicate a previous instance of financing to all parties, and the double financing would be avoided. Oliver Wyman and Euroclear (2016) point out the possibility of placing invoices on the Blockchain in order to create a more reliable source of value to be used as collateral or as a demonstration of worthiness (p. 7).

For example, the London-based startup Tallysticks is creating a network where their Blockchain-driven application permits companies to automatically reconcile invoices, increasing accountability and efficiency. Because the invoices are tokenized in a Blockchain, they can be factored more easily since they are approved by the buyer and uniquely identified. Investors who finance the invoices could be sure that they are not previously sold or fake, reducing risk and therefore the cost of financing. It is therefore important to point out that a tokenised invoice results from the active participation of the commercial partners (i.e. suppliers and buyers) that have to cryptographically sign the invoice document on a Blockchain. For this reason, the solution strongly depends on the broad participation in the network. Invoices created by this mechanism can then be factored.

The integration with the payment system is given by the ability of smart contracts to take control over an asset registered on a Blockchain (e.g. crypto-cash) and automatically trigger the payment. This solution is proposed by Fluent Inc., a US-based startup, that aims to create a real-time payment platform for supply chain networks where all transactions are tokenised and pegged to fiat currency at a 1:1 ratio (Bauerle 2016, p. 27). Such a Blockchain-driven platform would integrate the payment and invoice layers, achieving faster and safer systems.

5.2.4   The Payment Layer

Developed to create 'a purely peer-to-peer version of electronic cash to allow online payments' (Nakamoto 2009), payments are the first application of BCT. With the use of Bitcoin or similar cryptocurrencies in a B2B scenario, buyer and supplier could transact without any intermediaries (e.g. banks) and with very small transaction fees. Although companies such as CVS, Amazon or WordPress already accept payment in Bitcoin,[4] Bitcoin and other cryptocurrencies are far from mainstream economy payment volumes. From the findings in Chap. 4, it can be assumed that throughput capacity and high volatility represent serious barriers to mass adoption and to serving B2B transaction volumes. As underlined by Yelowitz and Wilson (2015), users are still primarily computer programming enthusiasts and people driven by 'illegal' activities, and limited support exists for political or investment motives (pp. 3–6).

Blockchain technologies have instead found strong potential applications in the banking industry for improving the existing payment services (Accenture 2015, p. 13), particularly for international transactions and real-time payments (EBA 2015, pp. 11–13). This offers advantages for cross-border payments, for which transaction costs are relatively high. The use of smart contracts combined with a distributed ledger architecture could enable the real-time transfer of funds with minimal fees and guaranteed delivery without the need for correspondent banks or custodians (WEF 2016, p. 51).

Blockchain solutions could create more efficient payment processes between banks, eliminating the need for each institution to maintain and reconcile their own ledger. Fiat-pegged-cryptocurrencies are still in an early discussion stage, but they could radically improve the actual payment system. Andolfatto (2015) proposes a

---

[4]A full list can be found on http://www.bitcoinvalues.net/who-accepts-bitcoins-payment-companies-stores-take-bitcoins.html.

government-sponsored cryptocurrency where the exchange rate is pegged to the legal tender currency and where fiat-tokens will be guaranteed and issued by central banks.

5.3   Opportunities of Blockchain-Driven Supply Chains

Figures 5.5 and 5.6 sum up and illustrate a supply chain process driven by different technological solutions (i.e. with and without BCT). Trade document flow could be processed using the Blockchain as the underlying database layer, which will guarantee the authenticity and allow the straight through processing in the invoice approval. The traded goods are also uniquely identified and submitted to the custody of a smart contract that guarantees that a payment will be processed if certain events are satisfied (e.g. a successful shipping and invoice due date). Higher levels of trust in commercial relations, fast straight through processing and cheaper transaction costs could be the results of using the Blockchain.

We now try to define how the different use cases, which could be implemented in the different supply chain layers, can create opportunities for approved payables financing solutions. A set of opportunities have been identified and are discussed in the following subsections.

5.3.1   Increased 'Window of Opportunities'

Since SCF solutions rely on efficient and fast processing of supply chain data, the automation of processes is a key driver for the development of the SCF market (Camerinelli and Bryant 2014). A certain extent of dematerialisation and acceleration of processes is already offered by e-invoicing, which replaces the paper-based distribution and provides faster receipt of the document by the buyer. Certain forms of automation already exist with the self-billing procurement model, which can be deployed in the large ERP systems and simplifies the approval of payments due to electronic three-way matching. A back-end Blockchain system could further enhance the automation of such processes, since fully digital and signed delivery documents, such as 'bills of lading', would exist on it. The earlier the invoice is approved, the longer the time interval in which financing is possible (see Fig. 5.7). Blockchain-driven documentary trade processing could, in this sense, become the catalyst to establish a fully straight-through process (STP) and, thus, faster invoice approval.

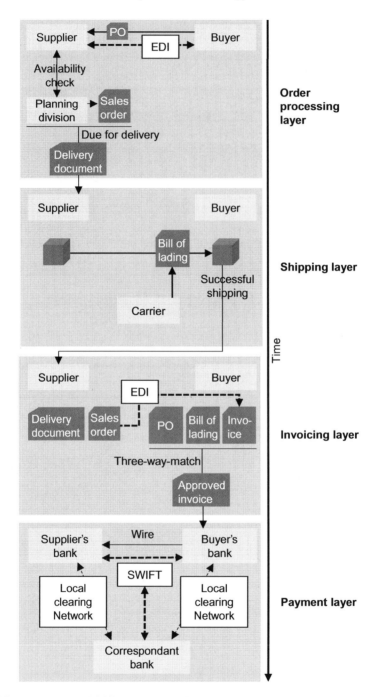

Fig. 5.5 Procurement and fulfilment process without BCT

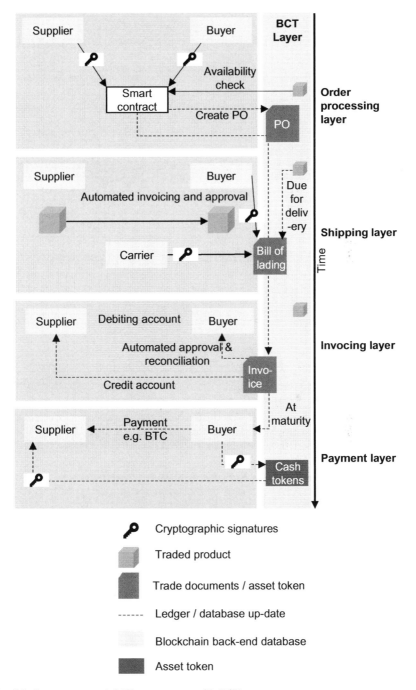

Fig. 5.6 Procurement and fulfilment process with BCT

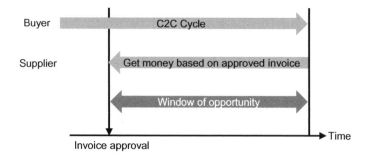

Fig. 5.7 The 'window of opportunity' (adapted from Camerinelli and Bryant 2014, p. 94)

5.3.2 Efficient Cash Settlement

An interesting feature is the opportunity offered by smart contracts to create a
one-layer invoice payment system. 'Smart invoices' could be paid automatically at
maturity to reduce manual intervention and ease the processes. Such possibilities,
however, already exist with modern ERP systems: payments can be made automatically via a payment program that retrieves all authorised invoices within a
specified timeframe and automatically generates payments (Magal and Word 2011,
pp. 4–35).

Also, if pure peer-to-peer payments (such as Bitcoin) are highly unlikely to be
deployed at B2B transaction levels, improvements offered by DLTs for the
bank-driven payment systems would allow faster cash settlement and lower
transaction fees with benefits for the entire SCF community. Multi-currency and
global supplier-base programmes would particularly benefit from lower transaction
costs in such a scenario.

5.3.3 Simplified Invoice Validity Check

Legal validity of invoices is a major issue for SCF programs. First of all, the buyer
has the risk of double payment in cases in which invoices were already sold to a
third party. Second, as the existence of undisclosed assignments in the purchased
receivables portfolio cannot be determined by the financing party, the risk needs to
be mitigated by a strong 'promise to pay' from the buyer. By assuring legal validity
through BCT, the 'promise to pay' can be phrased less strongly (what helps the
issue of accounting treatment), and the overall risk of the structure is reduced,
which helps all parties of the SCF program.

The legal validity issue also presents itself in supplier-led financing solutions
(e.g. factoring or receivables finance), because the buyer (debtor) is usually not

known by the financing parties. Because there are players in the market (e.g. banks) that are obliged by internal rules to perform checks on the legal validity of invoices, appropriately tokenised invoices would bring advantages for approved payables finance as well as supplier-led financing solutions. To be valid, an electronic invoice must be digitally signed, an element that is an integral part of every Blockchain solution.

5.3.4   Integration of Product and Money Flows

Being largely event-driven, SCF could strongly benefit from a technology that can create trigger points to key events in the physical supply chain. The combination of Blockchain and IoT solutions could offer the possibility to track the physical supply chain so as to adjust the risk at each step of the shipping process to fulfil the PO.

Tracking the product along the shipping process is already possible thanks to special devices that provide, for example, GPS, temperature or other relevant data to the interested parties in a trade transaction. The key features of immutable, tamper-proof and real-time data offered by a Blockchain solution could provide greater trust and availability to data consumers (e.g. banks involved in pre-shipment finance) and generate authoritative records for the execution of smart contracts and automation in the creation of trade documents.

The problem today is that perceived risk does not reflect the real risk profile because of the inability to track each step of the PO fulfilment process with sufficient granularity, resulting in fragmentation (see Fig. 5.8). The real risk profile could be illustrated as the composition of credit risk and performance risk, where the latter is related to the performance risk of the supplier in fulfilling the PO, and the credit risk is the credit quality (e.g. rating) of the buyer (Camerinelli and Bryant 2014, p. 82). The possibility to obtain information on goods to be despatched, conduct a pre-shipment inspection or obtain evidence of shipment can create data that could be matched with the PO and enable an automated adjustment of the performance risk. Performance risk also includes the willingness to pay from the buyer that depends on disputes caused by unmatched delivery versus PO.

As seen in the previous chapters, the trigger event in reverse factoring is the invoice approval, which allows the release of the funding against the approved payables. At this stage, the related risks depend only on the credit risk of the buyer, because the willingness to pay is confirmed (i.e. delivery is matched and payable approved), and any tracking information of the physical supply chain would become obsolete for this type of instrument. For this reason, integrating product and money flows is interesting only for SCF instruments that are triggered in the pre-shipment phase, such as inventory financing or PO financing.

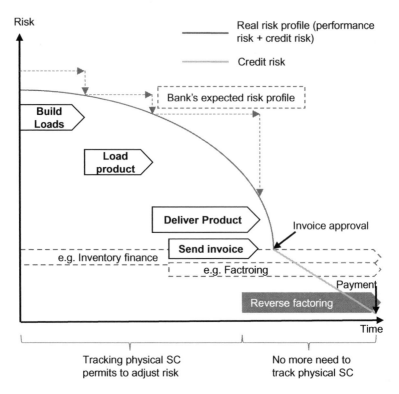

Fig. 5.8 Simplified risk perception in supply chain processes (adapted from Camerinelli and Bryant 2014, pp. 79–83)

5.4   Blockchain-Driven Reverse Securitisation

Figure 5.9 illustrates the principal opportunities that arise from the adoption of BCT in delivering a multi-investor reverse securitisation financing. As shown in the previous chapters, the use of a shared and trusted database layers can support the financing process, beginning with the programme setup until the key day-to-day operations, which include the invoice approval, note's issuance and related post-trade processes, payments and compliance activities (Fig. 5.9).

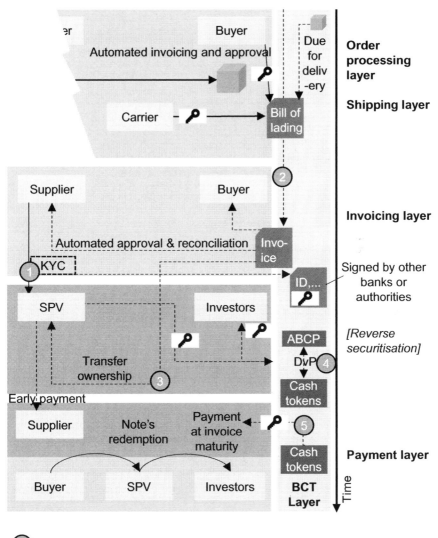

① Cost-effective supplier on boarding

② Straight-through trade document processing - faster invoice approval

③ Clear title of ownership and invoice validity

④ Efficient note issuance and clearing & settlement

⑤ Faster and cheaper payment systems

Fig. 5.9 Blockchain-driven multi-investor reverse securitisation

References

Accenture (2015) Distributed consensus ledgers for payments. https://www.accenture.com/t20151002T010405__w__/us-en/_acnmedia/Accenture/Conversion-Assets/DotCom/Documents/Global/PDF/Dualpub_22/Accenture-Banking-Distributed-consensus-ledgers-payment.pdf

Andolfatto D (2015) Fedcoin: on the desirability of a government cryptocurrency. http://andolfatto.blogspot.ch/2015/02/fedcoin-on-desirability-of-government.html

Bauerle N (2016) Trade finance and supply chains. CoinDesk, New York

Biella M, Zinetti V (2016) Blockchain technology and applications from a financial perspective: unicredit technical report. https://www.weusecoins.com/assets/pdf/library/UNICREDIT%20-%20Blockchain-Technology-and-Applications-from-a-Financial-Perspective.pdf

Camerinelli E (2016) Blockchain in the supply chain. Enrico Camerinelli

Camerinelli E, Bryant C (2014) Supply chain finance—EBA European market guide version 2.0. https://www.abe-eba.eu/downloads/knowledge-and-research/1406_EBA_Supply_Chain_Finance_European_Market_Guide_Second_edition.pdf

Deloitte (2016) Blockchain applications in banking. https://www2.deloitte.com/content/dam/Deloitte/uk/Documents/Innovation/deloitte-uk-Blockchain-app-in-banking.pdf

EBA (Euro Banking Association) (2015) Cryptotechnologies, a major IT innovation and catalyst for change: 4 categories, 4 applications and 4 scenarios version 1.0. https://www.abe-eba.eu/downloads/knowledge-and-research/EBA_20150511_EBA_Cryptotechnologies_a_major_IT_innovation_v1_0.pdf

ESMA (European Securities and Market Authority) (2016) The distributed ledger technology applied to Securities markets. http://www.the-Blockchain.com/docs/ESMA-DLT-Applied-to-European-Securities-Markets.pdf

GBST (2016) Four scenarios for blockchain capital markets. http://www.gbst.com/insights/gbst-insights/four-scenarios-for-blockchain-in-capital-markets

Goldman Sachs (2016) Blockchain: putting theory into practice. https://www.coursehero.com/file/16984495/Goldman-Sachs-report-Blockchain/

Gronau N (2004) ERP—Systeme—Architektur und Funktionen. http://wi.uni-potsdam.de/hp.nsf/0/5996B17E2C7754B6C1257147004BDFE4/$FILE/ERP-Systeme%20-%20Architektur%20und%20Funktionen.pdf

Gustin D (2014) Supply chain finance payable reclassification issue—dead or alive? http://spendmatters.com/tfmatters/supply-chain-finance-payable-reclassification-issue-dead-or-alive/

Harris P (2016). How blockchain technology is reinventing global trade efficiency. https://godistributed.com/ledger/26/

IBM (2015) ADEPT: An IoT practitioner perspective. https://www.scribd.com/doc/252917347/IBM-ADEPT-Practictioner-Perspective-Pre-Publication-Draft-7-Jan-2015

Lazanis R (2015) How technology behind Bitcoin could transform accounting as we know it. https://techvibes.com/2015/01/22/how-technology-behind-bitcoin-could-transform-accounting-as-we-know-it-2015-01-22

Kent (1987) In: Röthlin M (ed) Management of data quality in enterprise resource planning systems. Josef Eul Verlag, Lohmar Köln

Lawlor C (2016) Tokenization of invoices: a blockchain technology supply chain finance use-case. https://commercialfinanceassociationblog.com/2016/06/27/tokenization-of-invoices-a-Blockchain-technology-supply-chain-finance-use-case/

Magal S, Word J (2011) Integrated business processes with ERP systems. Wiley, Hoboken

McKinsey, Co (2015) Supply chain finance—emergence of a new competitive landscape. http://www.mckinsey.com/industries/financial-services/ourinsights/supply-chain-finance-the-emergence-of-a-new-competitive-landscape

Mainelli M, Milner A (2016) SWIFT working paper: the impact and potential of Blockchain on the securities transaction lifecycle. http://www.zyen.com/Publications/The%20Impact%20and%20Potential%20of%20Blockchain%20on%20the%20Securities%20Transaction%20Lif.pdf

Nakamoto S (2009) A peer-to-peer electronic cash system. https://bitcoin.org/bitcoin.pdf

Nassr I, Wehninger G (2015) Unlocking SME finance through market-based debt: securitisation, private placements and bonds. Financial Market Trends 2014(2):89–189

Oliver Wyman, Euroclear (2016) Blockchain in capital markets—the prize and the journey. http://www.oliverwyman.com/content/dam/oliver-wyman/global/en/2016/feb/Blockchain-In-Capital-Markets.pdf

Röthlin M (2010) Management of data quality in enterprise resource planning systems. Josef Eul Verlag, Köln

WEF (World Economic Forum) (2016) The future of financial infrastructure—an ambitious look at how blockchain can reshape financial services. http://www3.weforum.org/docs/WEF_The_future_of_financial_infrastructure.pdf

Yelowitz A, Wilson M (2015) Characteristics of Bitcoin users: an analysis of Google search data. Appl Econ Lett 22(13):1030–1036

Chapter 6
Discussion—How Does the Full Potential of Blockchain Technology in Supply Chain Finance Look Like?

Within this book, we suggest that blockchain technology (BCT) could lead to faster and cheaper supply chain finance (SCF) solutions. A trusted and shared underlying database that allows peers (i.e. SCF actors) to securely exchange trigger documents and assets directly on the Internet without the use of trusted third parties or time-consuming compliance checks represents a change of paradigm and offers new ways to operate at the business level.

As seen, one of the most important factors of successful SCF programmes is the improvement of software and technology solutions that allow businesses to come together in partnership and speed up cash flows throughout the supply chain due to the enhanced automation of processes. BCT has also enabled specialist financial technology firms to provide new platforms or software-based services to support SCF operations, which could facilitate the reconciliation process and the exchange of documents, payments, financial instruments and all related information.

6.1 A Wider Scope of Supply Chain Finance Solutions

For this section, the approach to identifying opportunities arising from the adoption of blockchain technologies is similar to the one used for approved payables financing techniques—identify the current issues and see how BCT could mitigate and eliminate them. Figure 6.1 shows a graphical illustration of our scope.

6.1.1 Blockchain-Based Inventory Financing

For inventory finance, the financing is usually confined to finished goods. In this case, the financing party provides funds against the inventory (as collateral) or by

E. Hofmann et al., *Supply Chain Finance and Blockchain Technology*,
SpringerBriefs in Finance, DOI 10.1007/978-3-319-62371-9_6

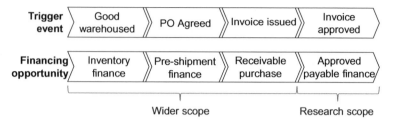

Fig. 6.1 Wider research scope along the supply chain process

way of a sale and repurchase agreement for the duration of the transaction (Camerinelli and Bryant 2014, p. 64). The financing need will depend on the structure and timing of the manufacturing and delivery cycles deployed along the supply chain (GSCFF 2015, p. 56). For example, this would not be the case for just-in-time production methodology but rather when goods are produced or bought and warehoused for a certain amount of time.

Principal differences

For these financing instruments, the intrinsic risk is higher than for invoice-based financing techniques due to the fact that the financing party is engaged in the very early stages of the transaction. The key risk factors are represented by high tradability and high durability (when possible with increasing value over time) of the inventory goods that are collateralised.

Contrary to all other SCF instruments, an underlying transaction between a supplier and a buyer is not necessary (Commercial Capital LLC 2015). Though, it is preferred if a buyer has already been identified (i.e. a PO has already been issued) in order to hedge the risk related to marketability and has thus secured a source of repayment (Camerinell and Bryant 2014, p. 64). For this reason, this financing solution can also fall under the umbrella of PO-based instruments. It is important, though, that the warehouse where the goods are stocked satisfies specific conditions that guarantee the quality over time. Therefore, the trigger event is not represented by the issuance of a commercial document, such as an invoice or a PO, but by the issuance of a warehouse receipt. Financial parties usually require agreements with a warehouse operator (logistics service provider) and third-party collateral management or inspection agents (GSCFF 2015, p. 58), and the financing does not cover 100% of the value of the collateral value (OECD 2015; Commercial Capital LLC 2015).

Typically, the financing party, an inspection company and the supplier will enter into a collateral management agreement (CMA) or a stock monitoring agreement (SMA) (ICC 2016). Under a CMA, the inspection company takes the physical possession of the goods, and, once the quality and quantity are inspected, it issues the warehouse receipt. This solution represents the highest security for the lending bank. Under an SMA, the inspection company does not take control of the inventory but regularly performs a physical inspection (i.e. audit) of it and compares the measurements with the warehouse receipt issued by the warehouse company or the supplier.

Issues

As seen, the continuous monitoring of the condition and value of the inventory needs specialised service providers, such as warehouse operators, that offer both depositor and lender certification and inspection services in order to ensure the warehouse meets necessary standards for safe and secure storage (OECD, p. 28). Because of the involvement of multiple third parties under different agreements, the ICC (2016) has identified a series of issues. Incorrect, unclear or forged storage documents could create the risk that the bank is financing an incorrect amount or non-existing goods. Risks also exist if the same goods have already been (intentionally) financed by another financing party (i.e. double financed). A clear match between documents and physical goods are also prerequisites for avoiding possible ownership disputes over the collateralized assets.

The 2014 Qingdao port scandal is one example of why auditing and due diligence processes are necessary for protecting not only the investors, but also the reputation of an ecosystem. In this case, a Chinese mining company and its subsidiaries used fraudulent warehouse receipts to borrow many loans from Chinese and foreign banks against a single deposit of metals stored at the Qingdao port. This resulted in high financial losses for banks and loss of reputation in the Chinese commodities industry.

For this reason, the inspection company in charge has so to perform time-consuming and costly manual tasks, such as proofing of the authenticity of storage documents, reconciling these documents with the warehouse ledger and physically checking quantity and quality of the goods. Ensuring visibility and transparency for high amounts of goods such as commodities may be a difficult task, but it is necessary in order to avoid fraudulent behaviours.

Furthermore, because of those high associated costs, in order to be economically viable, the minimum financing requirements is $500,000 (Commercial Capital LLC 2015), and, if combined with the constraint set by the type of goods that can usually be financed, only large commodity traders can benefit from this particular instrument.

Opportunities

Blockchain-driven activity registries could offer the opportunity to connect a vast array of users across the network in order to maintain the integrity of the warehouse status and receipt data and thus avoid forgery and 'double spending' issues. The technology creates an overlying layer upon the physical and financial world for a secure exchange and storage of trade related documents. Cryptographically signed by multiple parties and registered into the distributed ledger, the information will be available to interested parties, such as banks or customs authorities, so that they can rely on a single trusted source without involving any third party, such as auditors or inspection companies. Cases of fraud like the Qingdao port scandal might never have happened if the financing of the metal had been processed through a secure distributed ledger in which multiple copies of a shared single ledger are continually evaluated (Kynetix 2016, p. 4).

Another discussed set of use cases falls under the BCT capacity to act as asset registry in order to determine the title of ownership and act as 'digital notary' for the transaction of the digital represented assets. All the network participants are aware that a transaction of certain commodities, in this specific case, has taken place between a supplier and a financial provider for financing purposes. For example, Kynetix (kynetix.com), a London-based advisory company, successfully transferred the title of one lot food commodity by using Sentinel, an in-house Blockchain platform that links the financial markets to the physical economy through the creation of electronic records of title, ownership and commodity storage information.

Registering the asset on a distributed ledger could also trigger the smart contract feature in the case of sale and repurchase agreements. A smart contract embeds the terms of the loan agreement between the supplier and financing party and acts as escrows for the payment versus delivery, which could potentially take place as a straight-through-process, increasing speed and reducing costs and the probability of human errors.

Questions arise on how the physical goods are 'tagged' in order to be linked to the digital ones represented on the distributed ledger. The goods (or a lot of goods) must in fact be clearly identifiable in order to conclude that a specific token is really the digital representation of a specific physical good. For example, the start-up Everledger (everledger.io) links the physical diamonds with the unique data points of the stone and a laser serial number inscribed on it; Chronicled (chronicled.com), on the other hand, uses 3D-printed smart tags that are linked to the blockchain, giving a unique and immutable identity and chain of custody to limited edition sneakers.

Visionary or not, this is what a possible future in inventory financing could look like. The success will rely on the capacity of the industries to find the same standards and the willingness of the relevant parties to join the distributed ledger network, which for this type of use case will probably take the form of a consortium (Kynetix 2016). Faster and cheaper financing from the trust mechanism provided by BCT could create more stable SCF ecosystems.

6.1.2 Blockchain-Based Purchase Order Financing

In purchase order financing (PO finance), which falls under the umbrella of PO-based instruments, financing occurs before shipment of goods. The funds usually cover the working capital needs for the order's execution, such as raw materials, wages or packaging costs (Camerinelli and Bryant 2014, p. 61), and are paid directly to the supplier (who has received the PO).

Principal differences

Because the financing is provided at an early stage of the supply chain process, the costs for this type of instrument are higher (Commercial Capital LLC 2015; Universal funding 2013). Contrary to reverse factoring instruments, the buying party plays only a marginal role in the risk assessment, which defines the cost of financing. As pointed out in Camerinelli and Bryant (2014), because the funds are provided before shipment, the ability of the supplier to perform the order against the PO is the defining characteristic of this type of instrument (pp. 61–63). The creditworthiness of the buyers could in any case also be leveraged if they are large and well-rated companies (Universal funding 2013).

There are other differences regarding restrictions on the type of order—because of the higher inherent risk, this type of financing is usually limited to drop-shipping[1] orders with a required profit margin of 20% (Universal funding 2013; Commercial Capital LLC 2015).

For cross-border transactions, it is also common to issue a standard letter of credit (L/C) to secure the transaction, one in favour of the supplier's manufacturers (Commercial Capital LLC 2015; A/R Cashflow, n.d.) and another in order to mitigate the risk of non-payment by the buyer after successful delivery (Camerinelli and Bryant 2014, p. 63). The extensive use of this credit instrument represents another difference in approved payables financing solutions, which rely instead on open book accounting (O/A) terms.

Issues

The principal issues are presented by the time-consuming tasks that arise from creating transparency along the supply chain processes, from knowing the manufacturer (in case of drop-shipping) to ensuring data provided by the supplier is correct and that the location of goods and the shipping status is always known so that the order will be accepted with a high probability. This is usually done by engaging trusted third parties, such as auditors or logistics companies (A/R cashflow, n.d.), which increase the cost of finance. Even with the latest technological possibilities, this process continues to be associated with high effort, and, for this reason, PO financing is usually processed only in combination with trade finance instruments, such as a L/C, which creates additional costs during the transaction.

---

[1]This means that the suppliers, typically wholesalers, place the order for already finished goods (e.g. electronics or beverages), which are shipped from the producing company directly to the buyer.

Opportunities

We have already stressed that one of the advantages created by BCT-driven trade document issuance is the creation of unique and immutable data that is cryptographically signed by more entities and linked to a specific trade document. This data can be a hash of the document's information or a set of arbitrary data, such as PO number or amount, for example.[2] The financing party, then, could be sure of the authenticity of the document and that an identified buying party really exists. Checking the validity of the document through time-consuming manual intervention could then be avoided and could permit a high level of STP. Furthermore, similar to blockchain-driven invoice factoring, the possibility of the same PO being financed twice (i.e. double spent) could be avoided by consulting an authoritative ledger (i.e. a blockchain) that registers all financing transactions related to a given document. The pointing PO's hash is unique and is linked only to a single financing transaction.

Despite arguments against its validity,[3] another opportunity could arise from the IoT use, which creates the possibility to track the physical flow of goods along the supply chain. Every interaction with third parties or data related to the state of the goods shipped will be registered in a shared ledger so that chain of custody could be tracked and data could be compared with customs documents.

Registering this data in a blockchain opens up the possibility for smart contracts to read the relevant information in order to automatically process the payment related to a specific commercial transaction. As already pointed out in the previous chapter, it is important that the information inputs used by smart contracts derive from a state that is agreed upon by the whole network (i.e. submitted to a blockchain consensus protocol). Examples of authoritative values provided without BCT are, for example the Nasdaq or the LIBOR indices, which are universally accepted and could also act as oracles for smart contracts. BCT could establish an authoritative record for trade data and information in order to create trigger points for smart contracts. Furthermore, a smart contract would, for example guarantee that a buyer will pay if goods are successfully shipped within the terms agreed upon in the smart contract. This practice would strongly mitigate counterparty risks in commercial or financial transactions and probably avoid the costly paper-based issuance of a L/C actually deployed in PO financing.

---

[2]Arbitrary data (max 40 bytes) can be recorded in the transaction output of OP_RETURN, a script code used to mark a transaction in the Bitcoin blockchain (en.bitcoi.it 2015).

[3]Personal discussions about this topic always point out how reliable and useful it could be to create a digital reference in a blockchain of an object that already exists in the physical world, seeing that the tag or any device used to link it to the distributed database can be tampered or forged.

6.1.3 Blockchain-Based Receivables Financing

This supply chain downstream financing technique falls under the umbrella of the invoice-based instruments—most precisely, the supplier-led ones. The programme is set up to finance the receivables of the supplier (any), and the counterparty (i.e. the buyer) is usually not informed of the sale of the invoice. The classical factoring or forfeiting instruments also fall under this category and account for approximately 80% of the SCF invoice-based market.

Principal differences

Contrary to the buyer-led programmes, the liquidity is not provided by the initiative of the buying party, and the risk is therefore highly influenced by the creditworthiness of the supplier. Thus, compared to reverse factoring, the financing costs are usually higher if the supplier's credit rating is worse than the buyer's credit rating. Although, in both the cases of supplier-led and buyer-led programmes, the financial intermediary provides the funds by purchasing the receivables (i.e. the invoice with the embedded rights); in receivables finance, the funder has to evaluate the creditworthiness of each single supplier and each single buyer in order to price and accept the financing.

Issues

Contrary to reverse factoring, where the payables are approved by buyers and the payments only depend on the buyer's credit default risk, for receivables financing, a number of manual and time-consuming tasks (e.g. inspections by sampling) need to be performed in order to prevent fraud and losses. Camerinelli and Bryant (2014) identified the following issues and key risks:

- The invoice is presented to the bank before the goods are shipped. This increases the performance risks of the transaction, which is difficult for the bank to assess.
- The bank is unaware of a credit note issued together with the invoice.
- There are commercial disputes between commercial parties of which the bank is unaware.
- There are forged invoices where the amount has been modified or a false invoice for which a debtor does not even exist.

Furthermore, it is also possible that the same invoice is presented to different banks (i.e. double spent), which could lead to systemic risks in the SCF space.

Opportunities

Opportunities for this type of instrument arise from the application of BCT in the invoicing layer as already described. As previously explained, the principal purpose of registering an invoice on a blockchain is to avoid fraud and double-financing issues in invoice discounting and factoring. Each invoice would be distributed across the network and, as is done for Bitcoin transactions, hashed and time-stamped in order to create a unique identifier. If a supplier tried to sell the same invoice again through the network, that invoice would show a previous instance of financing to all parties, and the double financing could then be avoided. Thus, invoices become a more reliable source of value to be used as collateral or as a demonstration of worthiness for financing purposes.

As already mentioned, the start-up Tallysticks is creating a network where their blockchain-driven application allows companies to automatically reconcile invoices, which increases accountability and efficiency. Because the invoices are tokenised in a blockchain, they can be factored more easily since they are approved by the buyer and uniquely identified. Investors who finance the invoices could be sure that they have not been previously financed or faked, reducing risk and therefore the cost of financing. It is, therefore, important to point out that a tokenized invoice results from the active participation of the commercial partners (i.e. suppliers and buyers) that have to cryptographically sign the invoice document on a blockchain. For this reason, the solution strongly depends on broad participation in the network and the adoption of the invoice reconciliation mechanism proposed by such solutions. Invoices created by this mechanism can then be factored and become a product of a blockchain-driven accounting system.

The first concrete implementation of this in the market can be seen in the partnership between Standard Chartered Bank, DBS Bank and Infocomm Development Authority of Singapore (IDA), who are developing a proof-of-concept for a blockchain-based invoice trading platform named *TradeSafe*.[4] In a first step, the invoice number and bill of lading number are used to generate a unique hash value that is stored on the distributed ledger. Because hashes are only a string of characters, the confidential details of the underlying invoice will not be visible to the whole network. Once the hash is recorded, the bank receiving the invoice attaches one of four processing states to that hash value. If another bank enters the same invoice data fields into the ledger, it would generate the same hash value, alerting the second bank to the fact that the invoice already exists on the ledger and has already been submitted for early financing. The platform can therefore ensure that the same invoice is not financed twice.

6.1.4   Sum-up of the Wider Scope

Table 6.1 presents the cases discussed in the previous sub-chapter in a structured manner. For each of the identified issues, the table summarises the solutions provided by the adoption of BCT.

---

[4]A simplified explanation of the functioning of this platform can be found in Boey and Chanjaroen (2016).

Table 6.1 Wider scope of blockchain-based supply chain finance solutions

Supply chain finance issues	Opportunities of blockchain technology
Inventory financing	
Incorrect, unclear or forged storage documents could create the risk that the bank is financing an incorrect amount or non-existent goods. Costly and continuous monitoring systems have to be deployed	Blockchain-driven activity registry could offer the opportunity to connect a vast array of users across the network in order to maintain the integrity of the warehouse status and receipt data and thus avoid forgery
Same goods are financed by multiple banks without their knowledge	Blockchain-shared database could avoid the 'double spending' issues
Tracking the ownership of the financed goods	Transfer of title using blockchain and smart contract features creates transparency and reduces financing risks
Purchasing order (PO) financing	
Involving trusted third parties such as auditors or contacting third-party logistic companies in order to gain transparency increases the financing costs	The blockchain layer creates transparency and could allow a straight through financing process that reduces related risks and costs
Tracking the physical flow of goods	The combination of blockchain and IoT solutions could offer the possibility to track the physical supply chain so to adjust the risk at each step of the shipping process to fulfil the PO
Receivables financing	
Preventing double spending and invoice forgery are highly onerous tasks	Blockchain creates uniquely and immutable documents that can be efficiently exchanged on the internet and used as a secure source of collateral

6.2   Limitations

After having discussed the results and summarised the first conclusions, there are some limitations that have to be considered concerning this research.

The fast evolving state of the technology and of the research that has characterised blockchain and distributed ledger technologies during the timeframe in which this book was written has broadened our scope. For example, public and open-source blockchain projects have different features and protocols than private ones, with potentially different implications for the use cases and applications for the researched SCF instruments. Because the private and public blockchain debate is still open to discussion, and a dominant DLT design for serving the mainstream economy has not yet emerged, our theoretical framework assumes the discussed use cases to be valid for every form that this technology will take in the near future.

Furthermore, the regulatory and legal barriers that limit the application of BCT have not been specifically considered. Being strongly regulated, the financial and jurisdictional fields in which SCF solutions are processed and implemented could shape our assumptions and the resulting opportunities. Examples could be the legal validity of smart contracts, as well the proof of ownership of asset tokens registered on shared ledgers.

Another cornerstone is the regulation and legal admission of fiat currencies in the blockchain (e.g. a 'Crypto-Euro'). Here, financial authorities are requested to provide the legal framework and the design for a technical infrastructure. Central banks have already recognised the huge benefits that the blockchain is able to provide. By offering tools like private and public blockchains and the provisioning of complete records of all transactions, BCT enables the financial authorities to get full read access, which therefore reduces the efforts of collecting transactional and statistical data, the management of central registers and the costly supervision of market participants. Although all the leading central banks, as well as legislative bodies like the European Commission, have started taskforces to explore and support the introduction of BCT, it will—based on the former legislation processes (e.g. electronic signature)—take some years until legal certainty will be achieved. Still, 'Once the general regulative framework of blockchain is in place, the adaption of BCT to SCF specific uses and processes like KYC, assignment of receivables, and transfer of securities should be feasible within a relatively short period of time as the existing legal environment offers sufficient legal flexibility', states Matthias Eggert (partner at Dentons and expert for SCF in the structured finance practice).

Limitations also arise from the scarce availability of proof-of-concepts (POCs) and data in order to strengthen the discoveries of this research, which is principally based on the most pertinent literature and working papers. Given the complexity and current stage of the technology, making any assumptions related to its costs of deployment in a SCF business scenario could result in a high level of approximation.

6.3 Future Research

Future studies in this nascent research field should be principally related to the limitations underlined in the previous section. Furthermore, as pointed out in the discussion, the scope should include all the SCF instruments that can be used along the supply chain. Future research could confirm our discoveries with a concrete business case or further explore the limitations of the applications with an analysis of the regulatory and legal frameworks.

Furthermore, the large number of potential commercial uses in the coming years will provide useful data that could be used to measure the impact on legacy SCF business models.

Gaps in the literature have been identified for reverse securitisation techniques in general. These gaps are assumed to be relevant, because this technique is substantially different from receivable securitisations and from standard asset-backed commercial papers (ABCPs). The instrument is also structurally different from the more traditional reverse factoring techniques due to the use of securitisation.

References

A/R Cashflow (n.d.) Purchase order finance. http://www.arcashflow.com.au/purchase-order-finance-white-paper-trade-finance.pdf

Boey D, Chanjaroen C (2016) StanChart, DBS's trade finance distributed ledger: how it works. In: Bloomberg Technology. https://www.bloomberg.com/news/articles/2016-05-22/stanchart-dbs-s-trade-finance-distributed-ledger-how-it-works

Camerinelli E, Bryant C (2014) Supply chain finance—EBA European market guide version 2.0. https://www.abe-eba.eu/downloads/knowledge-and-research/1406_EBA_Supply_Chain_Finance_European_Market_Guide_Second_edition.pdf

Camerinelli E (2015) Blockchain business scenarios. https://www.finextra.com/blogposting/11913/Blockchain-business-scenarios

Commercial Capital LLC (2015) How does purchase order funding work? http://www.comcapfactoring.com/blog/how-does-purchase-order-funding-work/

en.bitcoin.it (2015) Colored coins. http://coloredcoins.org/

GSCFF (Global SCF Forum) (2015) Standard definitions for techniques of supply chain finance. https://www.abe-eba.eu/Repository.aspx?ID=f7855005-f9b1-4b7e-bc4a-36ece3c9eb3b

ICC (International Chamber of Commerce) (2016) Inventory finance—the golden rules to mitigate legal risks. http://webcache.googleusercontent.com/search?q=cache:delx5ego3_MJ:www.iccwbo.org/Advocacy-Codes-and-Rules/Inventory-Finance-Golden-Rules-to-Mitigate-Risks/+&cd=1&hl=de&ct=clnk&gl=ch

Kynetix (2016) Improving confidence in the commodity markets. http://www.kynetix.com/wp-content/uploads/2016/04/Improving-Confidence-in-the-commodities-market.pdf

OECD (Organisation for Economic Co-operation and Development) (2015) New approaches to SME and entrepreneurship financing: broadening the range of instruments. http://www.oecd.org/cfe/smes/New-Approaches-SME-full-report.pdf

Universal funding Corporation (2013) Purchase order financing versus invoice factoring. http://www.universalfunding.com/files/PO_Financing.pdf

Chapter 7
Conclusion—What Can We Learn from Blockchain-Driven Supply Chain Finance?

Our main purpose was to discover possible opportunities for specific supply chain finance (SCF) solutions—approved payables (or buyer-led) financing techniques—triggered by the use cases offered by blockchain technology (BCT). After having described all the different SCF techniques and processes in order to identify the current barriers, bottlenecks and pain points, two questions were posed:

- How can the application of BCT help to overcome the barriers of SCF solutions?
- What are the opportunities offered by possible applications of BCT in supply chain processes?

Blockchain is a shared database that is secure and anonymous and allows the exchange of goods and documents in a secure way without the involvement of third parties or having to carry out time-consuming tasks for the sake of transparency in order to assess risks and avoid fraud. In a first step, the main barriers and pain points for the different actors involved in an approved payables financing programme were identified, and in a second step, specific BCT uses were applied to buyer-led SCF models.

Due to unsolved accounting treatments issues, buyers face the risk of reclassification of the payables (from trade payables to financial payables) submitted for financing purposes. Improving the working capital without impacting the leverage and loan covenants is one of the main drivers for strong buyers to initiate a reverse factoring programme, and, for this reason, it is of fundamental importance to avoid reclassification. Blockchain-driven corporate accounting can simplify the auditing processes so that more time could be made available to discuss and investigate the accounting treatment of financed approved payables. BCT can change the way transactions are processed and data is stored and shared, but it cannot change the accounting rules. However, BCT has the potential to ease the situation regarding the 'promise to pay'. The issue here is that some auditors see in an abstract guarantee an indicator for *reclassification*. The fact that BCT can eliminate double payment risk causes the 'promise to pay' to be less strong and therefore reduces the risk of

E. Hofmann et al., *Supply Chain Finance and Blockchain Technology*,
SpringerBriefs in Finance, DOI 10.1007/978-3-319-62371-9_7

reclassification. Still, BCT does not bring salvation to the open accounting treatment issues.

Another issue is the costly and time-consuming tasks required to fulfil the compliance requirements for onboarding the suppliers. This increases the financing costs and largely precludes the access to the programme by the long-tail supplier-base, which are usually SMEs with the greatest financing needs. A blockchain-based, cost-effective KYC check could allow the inclusion of the long-tail supplier-base as well. In this case, the necessary client's information is registered on the shared database in order to avoid the occurrence in which the same client is singularly checked by multiple banks. Multi-bank SCF solutions could particularly benefit from this, since each bank has to perform the KYC checks independently. A shared and trusted KYC registry could encourage banks to participate in SCF programmes, increasing competition and thus providing better financing rates.

The last main issue is represented by the high transaction costs incurred from reverse securitisation techniques related to the post-trade processes. Custodian banks, clearing institutions and information services are necessary in order to permit the ABCP financing. BCT could be leveraged in order to allow transactions to be performed directly between peers—the supply chain actors. Near real-time settlement will permit more eligible payments for the programme because of the extended interest period, and the higher risk will make short-term securities more attractive for investors. In general terms, a faster securities settlement that is blockchain-based and cost-effective means lower transaction costs for investors, lower financing costs for suppliers, more participating suppliers and the resulting higher working capital gains for buyers.

In a third step, we analysed possible opportunities arising from the applications of this technology in supply chain processes. Being strictly related to the supply chain trigger events, SCF processes could be impacted by the use of this technology in the transaction and issuance of trade related documents or the possibility to create an overlying information technology that would allow faster payments and the ability to track the flow of goods.

Pure peer-to-peer payments are highly unlikely to be deployed at B2B transaction levels and at the volumes required by SCF solutions. If deployed, the faster and leaner cash settlements would lower transaction fees, with benefits for the entire SCF community. Multi-currency supplier-base programmes could particularly benefit from lower transaction costs offered by an adoption of blockchain solutions for international wire transfers. Furthermore, BCT offers the possibility to automatically perform payments based on information registered on the shared ledger as a result of smart contract-driven trade transactions.

Blockchain-driven solutions could also mitigate the risk of fraud and double financing by creating a unique invoice identifier database. Banks could benefit from blockchain solutions by proofing the legal validity of an invoice, and blockchain-driven integrated order processing and invoicing could automate the creation of these documents and faster invoice approval, extending the 'window of opportunities'. Furthermore, BCT could allow faster invoice processing and reconciliation, which will widen the range of opportunities provided by early payments to the suppliers.

Being largely event-driven, the combination of blockchain and IoT-driven solutions could offer the possibility to track the physical supply chain and provide trigger points to key events for a range of SCF solutions, such as inventory finance, pre-shipment finance or receivables finance. Approved payables financing instruments could only marginally benefit from this use, as they are located at the end of the supply chain process.

After having discussed the opportunities for approved payables financing, it was clear that a broader space for opportunities exists for SCF instruments that are triggered earlier in the supply chain. For these instruments, the risks are higher, and the visibility of the physical flow of goods is a key element of an effective SCF, for which blockchain offers interesting uses. For this reason, we widened the scope of the research to also analyse the other principal SCF techniques. The findings suggest that SCF finance instruments could broadly take advantage of the different uses offered by blockchain technologies. This is due to the enhanced trust that is created and the opportunity to securely exchange documents whose authenticity is certain by the possibility of tracking the inventory through ownership and supply chain trigger points or by the possibility of forming trade relations that are established under the custody of blockchain-enabled smart contracts.

Despite a growing number of startups that offer blockchain-based solutions and high venture capital (VC) funding in the crypto-space, the technology still sees niche commercial deployment but promises to change the way corporations and individuals exchange value and information over the Internet, allowing unprecedented levels of collaboration. With our book, we hope to have made a modest contribution to pave the way for all of the promising potential of BCT applications in SCF.

Printed in Great Britain
by Amazon